EDITOR: Maryanne Blacker
FOOD EDITOR: Pamela Clark

• • •

DESIGNER: Robbylee Phelan

• • •

DEPUTY FOOD EDITOR: Jan Castorina
HOME ECONOMISTS: Jane Ash, Tikki Durant,
Sue Hipwell, Karen Maughan, Voula Mantzouridis,
Louise Patniotis, Kathy Wharton
EDITORIAL COORDINATOR: Elizabeth Hooper
KITCHEN ASSISTANT: Amy Wong

• • •

STYLISTS: Rosemary de Santis,
Carolyn Fienberg, Michelle Gorry, Jacqui Hing,
Anna Phillips, Jenny Wells, Jon Allen
PHOTOGRAPHERS: Kevin Brown, Robert Clark,
Paul Clarke, Andre Martin, Robert Taylor,
Justine Kerrigan, Georgia Moxham

• • •

HOME LIBRARY STAFF
ART DIRECTOR: Paula Wooller
EDITORIAL COORDINATOR: Fiona Nicholas

• • •

PUBLISHER: Richard Walsh
DEPUTY PUBLISHER: Nick Chan

• • •

Produced by The Australian Women's Weekly Home Library.
Typeset by ACP Color Graphics Pty Ltd.
Printed by Times Printers Pte. Ltd, Singapore.
Published by ACP Publishing Pty Ltd, 54 Park Street, Sydney.

• • •

♦ **U.S.A.:** Distributed for Whitecap Books Ltd by
Graphic Arts Center Publishing, 3019 N.W. Yeon,
Portland, OR, 97210. Tel: 503-226-2402. Fax: 530-223-1410.

♦ **CANADA:** Distributed in Canada by Whitecap Books Ltd,
1086 West 3rd St, North Vancouver BC V7P 3J6.
Tel: 604- 980-9852. Fax: 604-980-8197.

• • •

Vegetarian Cooking
Includes index.
ISBN 1 86396 014 7

1. Vegetarian Cookery. (Series: Australian
Women's Weekly Home Library).

• • •

COVER: Clockwise from top: Avocado and Garbanzo Bean
Salad, page 47; Belgian Endive and Fruit Salad, page 64;
Fruity Seasoned Bell Peppers, page 46.
OPPOSITE: From top: Sunflower Fruit Salad; Brown Sugar
Meringues with Carob Cream, page 76.
INSIDE BACK COVER: From top: Chili Vegetable Hot Pot
page 44; Potato-Crusted Lentil Hot Pot, page 46.
BACK COVER: Clockwise from top left: Apricot Spiral
Teacake, page 86; Minted Parsley Salad, page 72;
Spicy Vegetables in Crispy Baskets, page 32;
Snow Pea, Apple and Nut Salad, page 72.

VEGETARIAN COOKING

If you enjoy eating well, you will enjoy this book. We have taken a middle-of-the-road point of view, and based our recipes on vegetarian principles without being too strict. We naturally did not use meat, but included eggs and dairy products in many recipes. You can also introduce your family to vegetarianism by using our recipes as accompaniments to meat, chicken or fish.

If embarking on vegetarianism as a way of life, you need to research and understand foods to be sure your meals are balanced. We have used some ingredients that may be new to you; these are described in the glossary. And we show you how to prepare yogurt, bean sprouts, peanut butter, mayonnaise, soy milk and cottage cheese. Our recipes contain no salt. Instead, we used vegetable bouillon cubes and vegetable bouillon paste to boost flavors; these can be omitted, if you prefer.

Pamela Clark
FOOD EDITOR

2 SOUPS

8 SNACKS

18 LUNCHES

37 MAIN COURSES

60 ACCOMPANIMENTS

74 DESSERTS

83 HEALTHY DRINKS

85 BAKING AND MORE

102 SWEET TREATS

104 DINNER PARTY FOR 2

108 DINNER PARTY FOR 6

113 BUFFET DINNER FOR 20

118 MAKE YOUR OWN ESSENTIALS

121 GLOSSARY

125 INDEX

Soups

Vegetables are the natural basis of these delicious and popular soups. They adapt without fuss to all types, ranging from hearty family fare to stylish starters for a dinner party. Some of our recipes reflect influences from international cuisines; most are subtly enhanced by readily-available herbs.

VEGETABLE AND BARLEY SOUP

Soup can be made several hours ahead; keep, covered, in refrigerator. Recipe unsuitable to freeze. Suitable to microwave.

½ cup pearl barley
3 cups water
1 tablespoon vegetable oil
1 medium onion, chopped
1 clove garlic, minced
2 medium carrots, chopped
1 medium potato, chopped
1 stalk celery, chopped
14½oz can tomatoes
1 large vegetable bouillon
    cube, crumbled
3 tablespoons chopped fresh parsley

Soak barley in the water overnight. Heat oil in large saucepan, add onion and garlic, stir over medium heat about 2 minutes or until onion is soft. Add carrots, potato, celery, undrained crushed tomatoes, bouillon cube, undrained barley and water mixture. Bring to boil, reduce heat, cover, simmer about 15 minutes or until vegetables are tender. Stir in parsley just before serving.

Serves 4.

GARBANZO BEAN AND LEEK SOUP

Soup can be made a day ahead; keep, covered, in refrigerator. Recipe unsuitable to freeze or microwave.

2 cups (6oz) dried garbanzo beans
1 medium leek, sliced
2 medium onions, sliced
2 bay leaves
2 teaspoons chopped fresh thyme
2 teaspoons chopped fresh marjoram
2 tablespoons Vecon
8 cups water
1½ cups (¼lb) shredded cabbage
¼lb broccoli, chopped
2 stalks celery, sliced

Soak beans in water overnight, drain. Combine leek, onions, bay leaves, herbs, Vecon, water and beans in large saucepan. Bring to boil, reduce heat, cover, simmer 1 hour. Add cabbage, broccoli and celery, cover, simmer about 15 minutes or until vegetables are tender. Remove bay leaves before serving.

Serves 6.

GREEN BEAN AND COCONUT CREAM SOUP

Prepare soup close to serving time. This recipe is not suitable to freeze or microwave.

1 medium carrot
2 tablespoons (¼ stick) butter
2 teaspoons chopped fresh
    lemon grass
2 cloves garlic, minced
1 teaspoon grated fresh gingerroot
1 teaspoon ground turmeric
2 teaspoons ground coriander
2 fresh green chili peppers, chopped
2 green onions, chopped
½ cup chopped green beans
3 cups canned unsweetened
    coconut cream
½ large vegetable bouillon
    cube, crumbled
2 cups (¼lb) bean sprouts
3 tablespoons chopped fresh cilantro

Cut carrot into fine strips. Melt butter in large saucepan, add lemon grass, garlic and gingerroot, stir over medium heat 1 minute. Add turmeric and ground coriander, stir over heat further 1 minute. Add carrot, chili peppers, onions, beans, coconut cream and bouillon cube, mix well. Bring to boil, reduce heat, simmer, uncovered, 5 minutes. Stir in bean sprouts and cilantro.

Serves 4.

RIGHT: From top: Garbanzo Bean and Leek Soup; Vegetable and Barley Soup.

CURRIED BEAN AND MUSHROOM SOUP

Soup can be prepared 3 days ahead; keep, covered, in refrigerator. Soup can be frozen for 2 months. Suitable to microwave.

½ cup dried red kidney beans
½ cup dried black-eyed beans
2 tablespoons (¼ stick) butter
1 small leek, sliced
1 small carrot, chopped
¼lb button mushrooms, sliced
1 teaspoon curry powder
14½oz can tomatoes
3 cups water
1 large vegetable bouillon
** cube, crumbled**
2 tablespoons chopped fresh parsley

Place beans in large bowl, cover with boiling water, stand 1 hour, drain. Cook beans in large saucepan of boiling water about 25 minutes or until tender; drain.

Melt butter in large saucepan, add leek, stir over medium heat about 5 minutes or until leek is soft. Add carrot, mushrooms and curry powder, stir over medium heat about 1 minute.

Stir in beans, undrained crushed tomatoes, water and bouillon cube. Bring to boil, reduce heat, cover, simmer about 35 minutes or until beans are tender. Stir in parsley.

Serves 6.

SWEET POTATO AND LENTIL SOUP

Soup can be made 3 days ahead; keep, covered, in refrigerator. Soup can be frozen for 2 months. Suitable to microwave.

2 teaspoons vegetable oil
1 small onion, chopped
1 medium (10oz) sweet
** potato, chopped**
1 cup (7oz) red lentils
1 large vegetable bouillon
** cube, crumbled**
3 cups water

Heat oil in large saucepan, add onion, stir over medium heat about 2 minutes or until onion is soft. Add remaining ingredients, bring to boil, reduce heat, cover, simmer about 20 minutes or until potato is soft. Blend mixture in several batches until smooth, return to saucepan, reheat before serving. Serve with plain yogurt, if desired.

Serves 4.

CREAM OF BROCCOLI SOUP

Soup can be made a day ahead; keep, covered, in refrigerator. Recipe unsuitable to freeze. Suitable to microwave.

3oz (¾ stick) butter
2 medium onions, chopped
½ cup whole-wheat flour
6 cups water
1 tablespoon Vecon
1½lb broccoli, chopped
1 medium tomato, chopped
1 teaspoon chopped fresh thyme
½ teaspoon chopped fresh rosemary
¼ teaspoon ground nutmeg
2 tablespoons fresh lemon juice
1 cup milk
¾ cup plain yogurt

Melt butter in large saucepan, add onions, stir over medium heat about 3 minutes or until onions are soft. Stir in flour, stir over medium heat 1 minute. Gradually stir in water, Vecon, broccoli, tomato, thyme, rosemary, nutmeg and juice, bring to boil, stirring. Reduce heat, cover, simmer about 15 minutes or until broccoli is tender. Blend mixture in several batches until smooth, add milk and yogurt, return to saucepan, reheat without boiling.

Serves 6.

ABOVE: Green Bean and Coconut Cream Soup.
RIGHT: From top: Curried Bean and Mushroom Soup; Cream of Broccoli Soup.

TOMATO AND PASTA SOUP

We used whole-wheat twisted pasta sticks for this recipe. Soup can be made a day ahead; keep, covered, in refrigerator. This recipe is unsuitable to freeze. Suitable to microwave.

1 tablespoon butter
1 medium onion, chopped
1 clove garlic, minced
2 cups water
1 large vegetable bouillon
    cube, crumbled
5 medium (1lb) tomatoes, chopped
3 tablespoons tomato paste
2 tablespoons chopped fresh basil
3oz whole-wheat pasta

Melt butter in large saucepan, add onion and garlic, stir over medium heat about 2 minutes or until onion is soft. Add water, bouillon cube, tomatoes, tomato paste and basil. Bring to boil, reduce heat, cover, simmer about 20 minutes or until tomatoes are cooked.

Add pasta gradually to large saucepan of boiling water, boil, uncovered, about 8 minutes or until pasta is tender, drain. Blend or process tomato mixture in several batches until smooth, stir in pasta. Serves 4.

CHUNKY VEGETABLE SOUP

Soup can be made a day ahead; keep, covered, in refrigerator. Recipe unsuitable to freeze. Suitable to microwave.

3 tablespoons butter
1 medium leek, sliced
¼ cup all-purpose flour
5 cups water
1 large vegetable bouillon
    cube, crumbled
¾lb broccoli, chopped
2 medium carrots, chopped
4 medium zucchini, chopped
1 small red bell pepper, chopped

Melt butter in large saucepan, add leek, stir over medium heat about 5 minutes or until leek is soft. Stir in flour, stir over medium heat 1 minute. Stir in water and bouillon cube, stir over high heat until mixture boils and thickens.

Add vegetables, cover, simmer about 10 minutes or until vegetables are tender. Serves 4.

RIGHT: Back, from left: Sweet Potato and Lentil Soup; Chunky Vegetable Soup. Front: Tomato and Pasta Soup.

Snacks

Making snack decisions will be a pleasure with our treats for different times and occasions. There are tasty light nibbles, child-pleasing snacks for school and after, picnic treats and dinner party appetizers. Some can be made ahead; others are best prepared just before serving.

TROPICAL MIX

Tropical mix can be made a week ahead; keep, covered, in refrigerator. This recipe is not suitable to freeze or microwave.

½ cup chopped dried apricots
½ cup chopped dates
½ cup golden raisins
¼ cup flaked coconut
¼ cup slivered almonds
¼ cup rolled rice
3 tablespoons vegetable oil
2 tablespoons honey

Combine apricots, dates, raisins, coconut, almonds and rice in large heatproof bowl. Combine oil and honey in small saucepan, bring to boil, boil 1 minute. Pour honey mixture over fruit mixture; mix well. Spoon tropical mix into shallow roasting pan, bake in 350°F oven 10 minutes, stirring occasionally; cool.

Makes about 2 cups.

ABOVE: Tropical Mix.
RIGHT: Frozen Fruit Pops

FROZEN FRUIT POPS

Ice block molds are available from large department stores. You will need about 4 passion fruit for this recipe. Pops can be frozen for 2 weeks.

½lb strawberries, sliced
¼ cup passion fruit pulp
2 teaspoons grated orange zest
½ cup fresh orange juice

Combine all ingredients in bowl. Spoon mixture into ice block molds, cover with lids. Freeze pops for several hours or overnight.

Makes 12.

NUTTY AVOCADO SPREAD

Spread is best made just before serving. Recipe unsuitable to freeze.

1 small ripe avocado, chopped
1 tablespoon fresh lemon juice
1 hard-boiled egg
¼ cup Brazil nuts, finely chopped
3 green onions, finely chopped
2 tablespoons chopped fresh parsley

Blend or process avocado and juice until smooth. Push egg through sieve. Combine avocado mixture, egg, nuts, onions and parsley in medium bowl, stir until well combined. Use avocado mixture as a sandwich spread.

Makes about 1 cup.

PUMPKIN SQUASH AND PEANUT BUTTER ROLLS

Rolls are best prepared as close to serving time as possible. Recipe unsuitable to freeze.

1 cup grated raw pumpkin squash
½ cup chopped celery
1 cup shredded lettuce
2 green onions, chopped
4 pieces lavash bread
½ cup smooth peanut butter

Combine squash, celery, lettuce and onions in large bowl, mix well. Spread 1 side of bread evenly with peanut butter. Divide squash mixture into 4 portions, sprinkle evenly over peanut butter. Roll bread up from narrow sides, cut into slices before serving.

Serves 4.

CAROB FRUIT SKEWERS

Skewers can be made several hours ahead; keep, covered, in refrigerator. Recipe unsuitable to freeze. Suitable to microwave.

3½oz milk carob, chopped
1 teaspoon vegetable oil
2 medium bananas
¾ cup crushed mixed nuts
½lb strawberries, halved
2 medium kiwifruit, chopped

Place carob and oil into small heatproof bowl, place over small pan of simmering water until melted. Cut each banana into 8 slices, dip slices into carob mixture, toss in nuts, place onto trays, allow to set. Alternate pieces of coated banana, strawberries and kiwifruit on wooden skewers.

Serves 4.

BELOW: Carob Fruit Skewers.
LEFT: From top: Nutty Avocado Spread; Pumpkin Squash and Peanut Butter Rolls.

CREAMED SPINACH PATE

Pate can be made a day ahead; keep, covered, in refrigerator. Recipe unsuitable to freeze or microwave.

2 bunches (2½lb) spinach
¼ cup water
1 large vegetable bouillon
 cube, crumbled
1 teaspoon ground nutmeg
1 teaspoon cornstarch
1 teaspoon water, extra
2 tablespoons (¼ stick) butter
1 large onion, chopped
2 cloves garlic, minced
¼ cup heavy cream

Combine spinach, water, bouillon cube and nutmeg in large saucepan. Bring to boil, reduce heat, simmer, uncovered, about 20 minutes, stirring occasionally, until liquid has evaporated and spinach is almost dry. Blend cornstarch with extra water, add to pan, stir over medium heat until mixture boils; cool.

Melt butter in medium saucepan, add onion and garlic, stir over medium heat about 3 minutes or until onion is soft, cool. Blend or process spinach mixture with onion mixture and cream until smooth. Transfer mixture to serving dish, cover; refrigerate several hours or until firm.

TOMATO AND ONION PITA PIZZAS

Recipe unsuitable to freeze or microwave.

4 whole-wheat pita pocket breads
½ cup bottled pasta sauce
1 cup (¼lb) grated cheddar cheese
2 medium tomatoes, thinly sliced
1 medium onion, thinly sliced
¼ cup pitted black olives, halved

Place pocket breads on baking sheet. Spread each pocket bread with pasta sauce, top with half the cheese, then the tomatoes, onion and olives, sprinkle with remaining cheese. Bake in 400°F oven about 15 minutes or until lightly browned.
Makes 4.

HUMMUS ALFALFA POCKETS

Hummus can be made 2 days ahead. Pockets best filled just before serving. Recipe unsuitable to freeze.

2 x 15oz cans garbanzo
  beans, drained
1 clove garlic, minced
1 teaspoon grated lime zest
2 teaspoons fresh lime juice
2 tablespoons chopped fresh oregano
¼ teaspoon tabasco sauce
1 teaspoon grated fresh gingerroot
2 tablespoons water, approximately
8 whole-wheat pita pocket breads
6 medium tomatoes, chopped
alfalfa sprouts

Blend or process garbanzo beans, garlic, zest, juice, oregano, sauce and gingerroot until smooth. Add enough water to hummus mixture to make a paste consistency. Divide hummus between pocket breads, top with tomatoes and alfalfa sprouts.
Makes 8.

SWEET CORN WAFFLES WITH CHUTNEY AND SALAD

Waffles can be frozen for 2 months. Salad unsuitable to freeze. Recipe unsuitable to microwave.

1 cup whole-wheat flour
¾ cup all-purpose flour
¼ cup self-rising flour
1 teaspoon ground cumin
1 tablespoon superfine sugar
2 eggs, separated
1¾ cups milk
¼ cup (½ stick) butter, melted
2 tablespoons water
1⅓ cups canned creamed corn
½ cup chutney

SALAD
1 Boston lettuce
1 medium carrot, sliced
1 small avocado, sliced
¼lb cherry tomatoes, halved
1 small green cucumber, sliced
¼ cup olive oil
¼ cup cider vinegar
1 teaspoon curry powder

Sift flours, cumin and sugar into large bowl, make well in center, gradually stir in combined egg yolks and milk, then butter, water and corn. Fold in softly beaten egg whites. Drop about 3 tablespoons of mixture onto waffle iron. Close iron, cook about 2 minutes or until golden brown. Serve waffles with chutney and salad.
Salad: Combine roughly torn lettuce leaves, carrot, avocado, tomatoes and cucumber in large bowl. Combine oil, vinegar and curry powder in jar, shake well. Pour over salad just before serving, toss gently.
Serves 6.

RYE SAVORY PIKELETS

Pikelet batter can be prepared 2 hours ahead; keep, covered, in refrigerator. Cook just before serving. Recipe unsuitable to freeze or microwave.

½ cup rye flour
½ cup self-rising flour
¼ teaspoon ground nutmeg
1 teaspoon sugar
1 egg, lightly beaten
1 cup milk, approximately
1 teaspoon cider vinegar
1 tablespoon butter, melted
½ cup grated cheddar cheese
¼ cup grated Parmesan cheese
3 tablespoons chopped fresh parsley
3 tablespoons sunflower seed kernels

Sift flours, nutmeg and sugar into bowl, make well in center. Gradually stir in combined egg, milk and vinegar, stir until smooth (or blend or process all ingredients until smooth). Stir in butter, cheeses, parsley and kernels. Drop dessertspoons of batter into heated greased heavy skillet, cook over medium heat until bubbles start to appear, turn pikelets, cook until golden brown on other side.
Makes about 20.

BELOW: Hummus Alfalfa Pockets.
BELOW LEFT: Tomato and Onion Pita Pizzas.
ABOVE LEFT: Creamed Spinach Pate.

WHOLE-WHEAT TARTLETS WITH MUSHROOM FILLING

Filling can be made a day ahead; keep, covered, in refrigerator. Recipe unsuitable to freeze. Filling suitable to microwave.

PASTRY
½ cup whole-wheat flour
½ cup all-purpose flour
3 tablespoons butter
1 teaspoon grated lemon zest
1 egg yolk, lightly beaten
2 tablespoons fresh lemon juice, approximately
⅓ cup grated cheddar cheese

MUSHROOM FILLING
2 tablespoons (¼ stick) butter
5 green onions, chopped
¾lb mushrooms, chopped
1 tablespoon all-purpose flour
¼ cup skim milk
¼ cup grated Parmesan cheese

Pastry: Lightly grease 12-hole tart tray (4 teaspoon capacity). Sift flours into medium bowl, rub in butter. Stir in zest, egg yolk and enough juice to mix to a firm dough. Turn pastry onto lightly floured surface, knead lightly until smooth, cover, refrigerate 30 minutes. Roll pastry out thinly, cut out 12 x 3 inch rounds, press into prepared pans, trim edges.

Cover each case with baking paper, fill with dried beans or rice, bake in 375°F oven 5 minutes. Remove beans and paper, bake further 5 minutes or until pastry is golden brown, cool. Place 1 rounded tablespoon of filling into each case, sprinkle with cheddar cheese. Bake in 375°F oven about 10 minutes or until cheese has melted.

Mushroom Filling: Melt butter in medium saucepan, add onions and mushrooms, stir over low heat about 5 minutes or until liquid has evaporated. Stir in flour, stir over medium heat 1 minute. Remove from heat, gradually stir in milk, stir over high heat until mixture boils and thickens; cool. Stir in Parmesan cheese.

Makes 12.

OLIVE CHEESE BITES

Cheese bites can be made several hours ahead; keep in airtight container. This recipe is not suitable to freeze or microwave.

½ cup all-purpose flour
½ cup whole-wheat flour
¼ teaspoon chili powder
3oz (¾ stick) butter, chopped
3 tablespoons grated cheddar cheese
3 tablespoons grated Parmesan cheese
2 teaspoons chopped fresh chives
1 egg, lightly beaten
24 large pimiento-stuffed green olives

Sift flours and chili powder into medium bowl, rub in butter. Stir in cheeses and chives, stir in enough of the egg to make a stiff dough. Press dough into a ball, cover, refrigerate 30 minutes. Roll dough out thinly on well-floured surface, cut into 24 rounds with a 3 inch cutter.

Rinse olives under cold water, drain on kitchen paper. Wrap each olive in a pastry round, place on baking sheet. Bake in 375°F oven about 25 minutes or until pastry is golden brown; cool on baking sheet. Serve warm or cold.

Makes 24.

CHEESY MILLET MUFFINS

Muffins can be frozen for 2 months. Suitable to microwave. Use microwave-safe muffin pan for microwave oven.

1 cup whole-wheat self-rising flour
1 cup millet meal
½ cup grated Parmesan cheese
3 tablespoons chopped fresh parsley
½ cup soy milk or milk
1 egg, lightly beaten
3oz (¾ stick) butter, melted
2 tablespoons hulled millet

Lightly grease a 12-hole cup cake pan (3 tablespoon capacity). Sift flour into large bowl, stir in millet meal, cheese and parsley. Make well in center, use a fork to stir in combined soy milk, egg and butter.

Spoon mixture into prepared pans, sprinkle with hulled millet. Bake in 375°F oven about 20 minutes or until lightly browned. Serve muffins warm or cold with butter, if desired.

Makes about 12.

RIGHT: Clockwise from top left: Sweet Corn Waffles with Chutney and Salad; Whole-Wheat Tartlets with Mushroom Filling; Olive Cheese Bites; Rye Savory Pikelets; Cheesy Millet Muffins.

ALFALFA BALLS WITH TAHINI SAUCE

Recipe can be made several hours ahead; keep, covered, in refrigerator. This recipe is not suitable to freeze or microwave.

6 slices whole-wheat bread, chopped
2 medium onions, chopped
1 cup (3½oz) walnut pieces
3 tablespoons arrowroot
1 teaspoon ground cumin
¼ teaspoon ground coriander
½ large vegetable bouillon
**   cube, crumbled**
1 cup (2½oz) alfalfa sprouts
2 teaspoons water, approximately
oil for shallow-frying

BROAD BEAN AND TOFU DIP

Dip can be made a day ahead; keep, covered, in refrigerator. Recipe unsuitable to freeze.

1lb fresh or frozen broad beans
½lb soft tofu, chopped
2 tablespoons fresh orange juice
2 tablespoons chopped fresh basil

Boil, steam or microwave broad beans until soft; cool. Remove skin from beans, discard skins. Blend or process all ingredients until smooth, spoon into serving dish; refrigerate 1 hour before serving. Serve with fresh crunchy vegetables.

Makes about 2 cups.

ABOVE: Broad Bean and Tofu Dip.
RIGHT: From left: Alfalfa Balls with Tahini Sauce; Curried Corn Fritters with Minted Sour Cream.

TAHINI SAUCE

½ cup plain yogurt
1 tablespoon tahini (sesame paste)
½ small green cucumber, chopped
1 teaspoon light soy sauce
1 tablespoon water

Blend or process bread, onions, walnuts, arrowroot, cumin, coriander and bouillon cube until smooth. Combine mixture with alfalfa sprouts in medium bowl, stir in enough water to bind mixture together (if necessary). Roll mixture into ¾ inch balls, shallow-fry in hot oil about 2 minutes or until golden brown, drain on absorbent paper. Serve hot with tahini sauce.

Tahini Sauce: Combine all ingredients in small bowl, mix well.

CURRIED CORN FRITTERS WITH MINTED SOUR CREAM

Batter can be prepared several hours ahead; keep, covered, in refrigerator. Fritters are best cooked just before serving. Minted sour cream can be prepared up to a day ahead; keep, covered, in refrigerator. Recipe unsuitable to freeze or microwave.

1 cup whole-wheat flour
2 teaspoons curry powder
2 eggs, lightly beaten
¾ cup milk
1 medium onion, grated
8¾oz can whole-kernel corn, drained
oil for shallow-frying

MINTED SOUR CREAM

1 cup light sour cream
2 tablespoons chopped fresh mint

Sift flour and curry powder into large bowl, make well in center, gradually stir in combined eggs and milk, mix to a smooth batter (or, blend or process all ingredients until smooth). Cover, stand 30 minutes. Stir in onion and corn. Shallow-fry tablespoons of batter in hot oil in medium skillet about 2 minutes each side or until golden brown. Drain on absorbent paper. Serve with minted sour cream.

Minted Sour Cream: Combine sour cream and mint in small bowl, mix well.

Makes about 20.

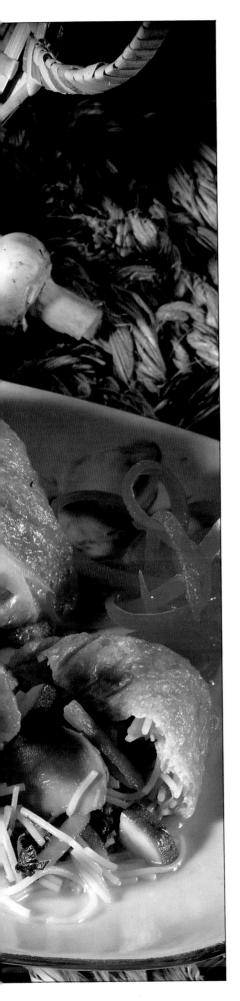

Lunches

We have plenty of fresh ideas about lunches, ranging from pastries to paella, croquettes and crepes and more. Variety is the key to enjoyment, whether you want a light meal or a hearty one. Some recipes can also be served as dinner party appetizers.

VEGETABLE TOFU POCKETS

Pockets can be prepared a day ahead; keep, covered, in refrigerator. Recipe unsuitable to freeze or microwave.

1 strip dried gourd
8 deep-fried tofu squares
3 cups water
1 tablespoon dashi concentrate
2 tablespoons teriyaki sauce
2 tablespoons dry sherry
TASTY VEGETABLE FILLING
2oz vermicelli noodles
3 medium Swiss chard leaves, chopped
3½oz oyster mushrooms, chopped
2 small carrots, finely chopped
2 small zucchini, finely chopped
¼ cup water
¼ teaspoon dashi concentrate
1 tablespoon teriyaki sauce
1 teaspoon dry sherry
½ teaspoon sugar

Cut gourd into 3 inch x 4 inch lengths. Place tofu squares and gourd strips into medium bowl, cover with boiling water; stand 15 minutes. Squeeze excess water from tofu, cut a thin strip from 1 edge of each square, pull cut edges apart to make pockets. Divide filling evenly between pockets, tie open edges with drained gourd strips.

Combine water, dashi, sauce and sherry in large saucepan, bring to boil, add tofu pockets; reduce heat, cover, simmer 15 minutes, lift carefully from liquid.
Tasty Vegetable Filling: Add noodles gradually to large saucepan of boiling water, boil, uncovered, 3 minutes, drain. Combine noodles with remaining ingredients in large saucepan, bring to boil, cover, simmer about 5 minutes or until vegetables are just cooked.

Makes 8.

LETTUCE PARCELS WITH CARROT SAUCE

Parcels are best prepared close to serving time. Carrot sauce can be made a day ahead; keep, covered, in refrigerator. This recipe is not suitable to freeze. Suitable to microwave.

5 medium potatoes
1 medium carrot, grated
2½ cups (7oz) shredded cabbage
2 tablespoons (¼ stick) butter
2 medium onions, chopped
2 cloves garlic, minced
¾ cup grated cheddar cheese
2 tablespoons sunflower seed kernels, chopped
1 tablespoon linseeds
3 tablespoons chopped fresh parsley
3 tablespoons chopped fresh cilantro
8 iceberg lettuce leaves
CARROT SAUCE
3 medium carrots
2 cups water
1 large vegetable bouillon cube, crumbled

Boil, steam or microwave potatoes until tender; drain. Mash potatoes in large bowl. Boil, steam or microwave carrot and cabbage until tender; drain, add to potato; mix well.

Melt butter in small skillet, add onions and garlic, stir over medium heat about 3 minutes or until onions are soft. Add to potato mixture with cheese, kernels, linseeds and herbs; mix well.

Drop lettuce leaves into large saucepan of boiling water, drain immediately; rinse under cold water, drain on absorbent paper. Divide potato mixture evenly over lettuce leaves, roll up firmly. Serve warm rolls with carrot sauce.
Carrot Sauce: Combine carrots, water and bouillon cube in medium saucepan, bring to boil, reduce heat, cover, simmer about 20 minutes or until carrots are tender. Blend or process until smooth, reheat if necessary.

Serves 4.

CHILI LENTIL LOAF

Loaf can be made a day ahead; keep, covered, in refrigerator. Recipe unsuitable to freeze or microwave.

1 cup (7oz) brown lentils
1 medium carrot, finely grated
1 stalk celery, chopped
2 small fresh red chili peppers, finely chopped
1 cup (2½oz) fresh whole-wheat bread crumbs
1 tablespoon tomato paste
1 medium onion, finely chopped
1 egg, lightly beaten

Lightly grease 5½ inch x 8 inch loaf pan, line base with baking paper, grease paper. Add lentils to large saucepan of boiling water, boil, covered, about 1 hour or until tender, drain; cool. Blend or process half the lentils until smooth. Combine all lentils, carrot, celery, chilies, bread crumbs, paste, onion and egg in large bowl; mix well. Press mixture into prepared pan, bake in 350°F oven about 1 hour or until firm to touch. Stand 5 minutes before turning loaf out.

Serves 4.

CARROT ZUCCHINI CROQUETTES

Croquettes can be prepared a day ahead. This recipe is not suitable to freeze or microwave.

2 large carrots, grated
1 large zucchini, grated
4 green onions, chopped
1 tablespoon chopped fresh cilantro
⅓ cup packaged ground hazelnuts
3 tablespoons whole-wheat flour
2 tablespoons (¼ stick) butter, melted
⅓ cup whole-wheat flour, extra
2 eggs, lightly beaten
2 tablespoons water
1 cup (2½oz) fresh whole-wheat bread crumbs
⅓ cup sesame seeds
oil for shallow-frying

Combine carrots, zucchini, onions, cilantro, hazelnuts, flour and butter in large bowl, mix well. Divide mixture into 10 equal portions, shape portions into croquettes. Toss croquettes in extra flour, shake away excess flour, dip in combined eggs and water, then combined bread crumbs and sesame seeds. Dip croquettes into egg mixture again, then in breadcrumb mixture. Place croquettes onto tray, refrigerate for 1 hour. Shallow-fry in hot oil until golden brown all over.

Makes 10.

RIGHT: Clockwise from left: Crepe-Wrapped Corn and Bean Loaf; Carrot Zucchini Croquettes; Chili Lentil Loaf.
ABOVE: Lettuce Parcels with Carrot Sauce.

CREPE-WRAPPED CORN AND BEAN LOAF

Unfilled crepes can be made up to 2 days ahead; keep, layered with baking paper, in refrigerator. Crepes can be frozen for 2 months. Corn and bean mixtures can be prepared a day ahead. Finished recipe not suitable to freeze or microwave.

CREPES
⅓ cup all-purpose flour
2 tablespoons yellow cornmeal
1 egg, lightly beaten
⅔ cup milk
1 teaspoon olive oil

CHILI BEAN LAYER
1½ x 8oz cans red kidney
    beans, drained
2 tablespoons tomato paste
1 small fresh red chili pepper,
    finely chopped
1 egg, separated
2 teaspoons chopped fresh oregano

CORN LAYER
11oz can whole-kernel corn, drained
1 teaspoon curry powder
1 egg, separated
2 tablespoons chopped fresh chives

Crepes: Line 3½ inch x 10½ inch baking pan with foil, grease foil. Sift flour into bowl, stir in cornmeal, make well in center, gradually stir in combined egg, milk and oil, mix to a smooth batter (or, blend or process all ingredients until smooth). Cover, stand 30 minutes. Pour 3 to 4 tablespoons of batter into heated greased small heavy-based crepe pan; cook until lightly browned underneath. Turn crepe, brown on other side. Repeat with remaining batter. You will need 6 crepes.

Line prepared pan with 2 crepes, trim crepes to fit. Spoon in bean layer, cover with 2 trimmed crepes. Spoon in corn layer, top with 2 crepes. Trim edges, cover loaf with greased foil, bake in 350°F oven about 5 minutes or until loaf is firm. Stand 5 minutes before turning onto wire rack. Carefully remove foil before serving loaf warm or cold.

Chili Bean Layer: Blend or process beans, tomato paste, chili and egg yolk until smooth, transfer mixture to medium bowl, fold in softly beaten egg white and chopped oregano.

Corn Layer: Blend or process corn, curry powder and egg yolk until smooth, transfer mixture to medium bowl, fold in softly beaten egg white and chives.

Serves 4.

ABOVE: From left: Mushroom Spinach Strudel; Crumbed Parsnip Sticks with Mustard Yogurt.

CRUMBED PARSNIP STICKS WITH MUSTARD YOGURT

Parsnip sticks and yogurt can be prepared a day ahead; keep, covered, in refrigerator. Deep-fry sticks just before serving. Recipe unsuitable to freeze or microwave.

3 medium parsnips
2 eggs, lightly beaten
¼ cup milk
3 tablespoons whole-wheat flour
2 cups (5oz) fresh whole-wheat
    bread crumbs
oil for deep-frying

MUSTARD YOGURT
1 cup plain yogurt
2 tablespoons seeded mustard

Cut parsnips into thin sticks, dip into combined eggs and milk, toss in flour. Dip sticks into egg mixture again, drain off excess, then toss in bread crumbs, pressing bread crumbs on firmly. Deep-fry sticks in hot oil in batches until golden brown and tender; drain on absorbent paper. Serve hot sticks with mustard yogurt.

Mustard Yogurt: Combine yogurt and mustard in a small bowl; mix well.

Serves 4.

MUSHROOM SPINACH STRUDEL

Strudel best prepared just before serving.
Recipe unsuitable to freeze or microwave.

8 medium Swiss chard leaves
2 tablespoons olive oil
10oz mushrooms, sliced
6 green onions, chopped
½ cup cottage cheese
¼ teaspoon ground nutmeg
1 egg, lightly beaten
6 sheets phyllo pastry
3 tablespoons butter, melted
2 teaspoons packaged unseasoned bread crumbs

Boil, steam or microwave Swiss chard until soft, squeeze out as much excess liquid as possible. Chop Swiss chard finely, place in medium bowl.

Heat oil in medium skillet, add mushrooms and onions, stir over medium heat until mushrooms are soft; drain. Add to spinach with cheese, nutmeg and egg, stir well; cool to room temperature.

Brush 1 sheet of pastry lightly with butter, top with another sheet of pastry, brush with butter. Repeat with remaining pastry and most of the butter. Spoon mushroom mixture along wide edge of pastry, fold sides in, roll up like a jelly-roll, place on baking sheet. Brush roll all over with remaining butter, sprinkle with bread crumbs. Bake in 375°F oven about 25 minutes or until lightly browned.

Serves 6.

BEANS AND PEPPERS WITH POLENTA TRIANGLES

Polenta can be prepared up to 2 days ahead; keep, covered, in refrigerator. Recipe is best made just before serving. This recipe is not suitable to freeze or microwave.

4 cups water
2 large vegetable bouillon
cubes, crumbled
1 cup (7oz) yellow cornmeal
oil for shallow-frying
½lb green beans
2 tablespoons (¼ stick) butter
2 medium red bell peppers, sliced
1 medium green bell pepper, sliced
¼ cup olive oil
2 tablespoons cider vinegar
1 clove garlic, minced
2 teaspoons chopped fresh basil

Lightly oil 7½ inch x 11½ inch baking pan. Combine water and bouillon cubes in large saucepan, bring to boil. Gradually add cornmeal to water, stirring constantly. Reduce heat, cover, simmer 30 minutes,

stirring frequently. Spread polenta evenly into prepared pan, cool; stand 2 hours. Cut polenta into 12 squares, cut each square in half diagonally.

Shallow-fry polenta in hot oil about 5 minutes each side or until golden brown.

Boil, steam or microwave beans until just tender, rinse under cold water. Melt butter in large skillet, add peppers, stir over medium heat 3 minutes. Combine oil, vinegar, garlic and basil with beans, add to peppers, stir over medium heat further 2 minutes. Serve with hot polenta.

Serves 6.

ABOVE: From top: Beans and Peppers with Polenta Triangles; Cheese Pasties with Tomato Basil Sauce.
RIGHT: Eggplant Chips with Pimiento Sauce.

EGGPLANT CHIPS WITH PIMIENTO SAUCE

Cook eggplant close to serving time. Sauce can be made up to 2 days ahead; keep, covered, in refrigerator. This recipe is not suitable to freeze or microwave. Sauce suitable to microwave.

2 medium eggplants
salt
cornstarch
oil for deep-frying

BATTER
1 cup self-rising flour
½ teaspoon chili powder
¾ cup water
2 eggs, lightly beaten

PIMIENTO SAUCE
1 tablespoon olive oil
1 medium onion, thinly sliced
1 clove garlic, minced
1 teaspoon cornstarch
¾ cup water
½ cup tomato puree
7oz can pimientos, drained, sliced

CHEESE PASTIES WITH TOMATO BASIL SAUCE

Pasties can be prepared a day ahead; keep, covered, in refrigerator. Recipe unsuitable to freeze or microwave. Sauce suitable to microwave.

1½ cups whole-wheat flour
½ cup all-purpose flour
½ cup self-rising flour
¾ cup (1½ sticks) butter
2 teaspoons fresh lemon juice
¼ cup water, approximately

RICOTTA CHEESE FILLING
¾ cup ricotta cheese
¼ cup grated Parmesan cheese
1 egg, lightly beaten
1 medium tomato, chopped
2oz button mushrooms, sliced
1 teaspoon chopped fresh basil
3 tablespoons chopped fresh parsley

BASIL SAUCE
1 tablespoon butter
1 medium onion, chopped
1 clove garlic, minced
14½oz can tomatoes
7oz button mushrooms, sliced
2 teaspoons sugar
2 tablespoons chopped fresh basil

Sift flours into medium bowl, rub in butter, add juice and enough water to make a stiff dough. Turn dough onto lightly floured surface, knead until smooth, cover, refrigerate 30 minutes.

Roll dough out on lightly floured surface to 14 inch x 18 inch rectangle, cut into 12 rounds with 4 inch cutter.

Place rounded tablespoons of filling onto center of each round, lightly brush edges with water, press edges together to seal, place onto baking sheet, prick top of pasties with fork. Bake in 400°F oven about 25 minutes or until lightly browned. Serve with sauce.

Ricotta Cheese Filling: Combine all ingredients in medium bowl, mix well.

Basil Sauce: Melt butter in small saucepan, add onion and garlic, stir over medium heat about 2 minutes or until onion is soft. Blend or process undrained tomatoes, add to onion mixture, stir in mushrooms, sugar and basil. Bring to boil, reduce heat, simmer, uncovered, about 5 minutes or until sauce thickens slightly.

Makes 12.

Cut eggplants into strips, place onto wire rack, sprinkle with salt, stand 30 minutes. Rinse eggplant under cold water, drain, pat dry with kitchen paper. Toss eggplant in cornstarch, shake off excess cornstarch, dip into batter. Deep-fry eggplant chips a few at a time in hot oil until golden brown; drain on absorbent paper. Serve hot chips with sauce.

Batter: Sift flour and chili powder into large bowl, make well in center, gradually stir in water and eggs, mix to a smooth batter (or blend or process all ingredients until smooth).

Pimiento Sauce: Heat oil in medium saucepan, add onion and garlic, stir over medium heat about 2 minutes or until onion is soft. Blend cornstarch with 2 tablespoons of the water, add to saucepan with remaining water, puree and pimientos, stir over high heat until sauce boils and thickens slightly.

Serves 4.

EGGPLANT SPREAD WITH LEBANESE BREAD

Spread can be made 2 days ahead; keep, covered, in refrigerator. Bread can be frozen for up to 2 months. Spread suitable to microwave.

1 large eggplant, peeled, chopped
salt
2 tablespoons olive oil
1 clove garlic, minced
¼ cup tahini (sesame paste)
2 tablespoons fresh lemon juice
¼ teaspoon paprika

LEBANESE BREAD
1 package (¼oz) active dry yeast
½ teaspoon sugar
1¼ cups warm water
2½ cups all-purpose flour
1 tablespoon olive oil

Place eggplant on wire rack, sprinkle with salt; stand 20 minutes. Rinse eggplant under cold water; drain well on absorbent paper.

Heat oil in medium saucepan, add eggplant and garlic, stir over low heat about 10 minutes or until tender. Blend or process eggplant mixture, tahini and juice until smooth. Transfer mixture to serving dish, sprinkle with paprika. Serve with crisp fresh vegetables and warm Lebanese bread.

Lebanese Bread: Combine yeast, sugar and water in small bowl, stir until sugar is dissolved. Stand in warm place about 10 minutes or until mixture is frothy.

Sift flour into large bowl, make well in center, stir in yeast mixture and oil, mix to a soft dough. Turn dough onto floured surface, knead about 3 minutes or until smooth and elastic. Return dough to large oiled bowl, cover, stand in warm place about 20 minutes or until dough has doubled in size.

Turn dough onto lightly floured surface, knead until smooth. Divide dough into 4, cover 3 pieces, roll remaining piece into 10 inch round. Place round onto lightly oiled baking sheet, bake in 400°F oven about 4 minutes or until puffed and lightly browned. Wrap in clean cloth, stand 3 minutes. Repeat with remaining dough.
Serves 4.

VEGETABLES WITH LEMON GINGERROOT SAUCE

Prepare recipe just before serving. Recipe unsuitable to freeze. Suitable to microwave.

½ cup blanched almonds
2 tablespoons vegetable oil
1 medium onion, chopped
2 cloves garlic, minced
1 medium green bell pepper, chopped
½lb green beans, chopped
¼ medium cauliflower, chopped
¼ small cabbage, shredded
2 medium zucchini, chopped
1 tablespoon cornstarch
¾ cup water
1 cup (2½oz) bean sprouts
¼ cup tamari shoyu
2 teaspoons fresh lemon juice
1 tablespoon grated fresh gingerroot
¼ teaspoon ground cardamom
1 tablespoon sugar

Toast almonds on baking sheet in 350°F oven about 5 minutes, cool. Heat oil in large wok or skillet, add onion and garlic, stir-fry over medium heat about 2 minutes or until onion is soft. Add pepper, beans and cauliflower, stir-fry about 5 minutes or until cauliflower is almost tender. Add cabbage and zucchini, stir-fry about 2 minutes or until cabbage is wilted.

Blend cornstarch with water, add to pan with sprouts, tamari shoyu, juice, gingerroot, cardamom and sugar, stir over high heat until mixture boils and thickens. Sprinkle with almonds just before serving.
Serves 4.

PASTA WITH TOMATOES AND CASHEW NUT BALLS

We used spiral pasta in this recipe. Sauce and cashew nut balls can be made up to 2 days ahead; keep, covered in refrigerator. This recipe is unsuitable to freeze. Suitable to microwave.

3 cups (1½lb) whole-wheat pasta

TOMATO SAUCE
2 tablespoons (¼ stick) butter
1 clove garlic, minced
1 large onion, chopped
4 large tomatoes, chopped
3 tablespoons tomato paste
2 teaspoons chopped fresh oregano
1½ cups water

CASHEW NUT BALLS
2 cups (10oz) unsalted, raw
    cashew nuts
2 eggs, lightly beaten
1 cup (2½oz) fresh whole-wheat
    bread crumbs
2 tablespoons olive oil

Add pasta gradually to large saucepan of boiling water, boil, uncovered, about 12 minutes or until just tender, drain. Serve hot pasta with tomato sauce and cashew nut balls.

Tomato Sauce: Melt butter in medium saucepan, add garlic and onion, stir over medium heat about 2 minutes or until onion is soft. Add tomatoes, paste, oregano and water, bring to boil, reduce heat, simmer, uncovered, about 20 minutes or until sauce is slightly thickened. Add cashew nut balls to sauce, reheat before serving.

Cashew Nut Balls: Blend or process nuts finely. Combine nuts, eggs and bread crumbs in large bowl, mix well. Shape mixture into 2¼ inch balls. Heat oil in skillet, add cashew nut balls, cook over medium heat about 3 minutes or until golden brown, drain on absorbent paper.
Serves 4.

VEGETARIAN PAELLA

Paella is best made just before serving. Not suitable to freeze or microwave.

1 tablespoon olive oil
1 clove garlic, minced
1 medium onion, sliced
1 cup long-grain rice
1lb broccoli, chopped
¼ medium cauliflower, chopped
14½oz can tomatoes
2 cups water
1 large carrot, finely chopped
1 medium red bell pepper, chopped
1 medium green bell pepper, chopped
1 teaspoon paprika
2 teaspoons chopped fresh oregano

Heat oil in large saucepan, add garlic and onion, stir over medium heat about 2 minutes or until onion is soft. Add rice, stir over medium heat 3 minutes. Stir in broccoli, cauliflower, undrained crushed tomatoes and water. Bring to boil, boil, uncovered, about 10 minutes or until rice is tender and most of the liquid is absorbed. Add remaining ingredients, mix well. Reduce heat, cover, simmer about 5 minutes or until peppers are soft.
Serves 4.

LEFT: Clockwise from top: Eggplant Spread with Lebanese Bread; Vegetables with Lemon Gingerroot Sauce; Pasta with Tomatoes and Cashew Nut Balls; Vegetarian Paella.

NUTTY MILLET AND RICE PILAF

Prepare pilaf just before serving. This recipe is not suitable to freeze or microwave.

1 tablespoon butter
1 medium onion, chopped
1 cup long-grain rice
¾ cup hulled millet
1½ cups water
**½ large vegetable bouillon
    cube, crumbled**
1 cup (¼lb) cooked green peas
¾ cup walnut pieces

Melt butter in medium saucepan, add onion, stir over medium heat about 2 minutes or until onion is soft. Add rice and millet, stir to coat grains with butter. Add water and bouillon cube, bring to boil, reduce heat, cover tightly, cook over very low heat 12 minutes. Remove from heat, add peas, cover tightly, stand further 15 minutes, stir gently with fork. Add nuts.
Serves 4.

SPAGHETTI SQUASH WITH BROCCOLI SAUCE

Recipe is best made close to serving time. Recipe unsuitable to freeze. Suitable to microwave.

4lb spaghetti squash

BROCCOLI SAUCE
1lb broccoli, chopped
1 medium carrot, chopped
1 medium onion, chopped
2 tablespoons (¼ stick) butter
1 tablespoon all-purpose flour
¾ cup milk
¼ cup plain yogurt
1 teaspoon French mustard

Cut squash into large pieces crossways. Steam or microwave squash until just tender, fork flesh away from skin to make spaghetti-like threads; drain. Serve with broccoli sauce.
Broccoli Sauce: Boil, steam or microwave broccoli and carrot until tender, drain.

Melt butter in medium saucepan, add onion, stir over medium heat about 2 minutes or until onion is soft. Stir in flour, stir over medium heat 1 minute.

Remove from heat, gradually stir in combined milk, yogurt and mustard, stir over high heat until mixture boils and thickens. Add broccoli and carrot, stir over low heat until hot.
Serves 4.

LEFT: Clockwise from top left: Vegetable Nut Crumble; Nutty Millet and Rice Pilaf; Spaghetti Squash with Broccoli Sauce; Tofu and Sesame Tartlets; Potato Croquettes with Dipping Sauce.

POTATO CROQUETTES WITH DIPPING SAUCE

Croquettes can be made 12 hours before serving. Sauce can be made a day ahead; keep, covered, in refrigerator. Sauce is not suitable to microwave. Croquette mixture suitable to microwave.

2 medium sweet potatoes, chopped
3 tablespoons butter
4 green onions, chopped
1/3 cup all-purpose flour
3/4 cup milk
3/4 cup grated cheddar cheese
2/3 cup fresh whole-wheat
   bread crumbs
2 eggs, lightly beaten
1/2 cup milk, extra
2 cups packaged unseasoned
   bread crumbs
oil for deep-frying
DIPPING SAUCE
1 cup white vinegar
1 cup superfine sugar
1 small carrot, grated
1 small green cucumber, chopped
2 tablespoons chopped fresh chives
1 small fresh red chili pepper,
   finely chopped
pinch paprika

Boil, steam or microwave potatoes until tender, drain well. Mash in large bowl until smooth, cool. Melt butter in small saucepan, add onions, stir over medium heat 1 minute.

Stir in flour, stir over medium heat 1 minute. Remove from heat, gradually stir in milk, stir over high heat until mixture boils and thickens, cool. Add onion mixture to potatoes, stir in cheese and fresh bread crumbs.

Spread mixture onto tray, cover, refrigerate until cold. Shape mixture into 16 croquettes. Dip croquettes into combined eggs and extra milk, then toss in packaged bread crumbs. Deep-fry croquettes in hot oil a few at a time until golden brown, drain on absorbent paper. Serve with dipping sauce.

Dipping Sauce: Combine vinegar and sugar in small saucepan, stir over heat, without boiling, until sugar has dissolved. Bring to boil, boil, uncovered, without stirring, about 3 minutes or until thickened slightly, cool 5 minutes. Pour over combined carrot, cucumber, chives and chili in a small bowl, cool. Sprinkle with paprika before serving.

Makes 16.

RIGHT: Asparagus Timbales.
ABOVE RIGHT: From top: Marinated Bean Sprout and Sesame Salad; Herbed Tomatoes with Cracked Wheat.

VEGETABLE NUT CRUMBLE

Crumble can be made a day ahead; keep, covered, in refrigerator.
Recipe unsuitable to freeze. Suitable to microwave.

1 cup brown rice
1/2 large vegetable bouillon
   cube, crumbled
1 egg
2 tablespoons (1/4 stick) butter
1 small onion, chopped
1 small red bell pepper, chopped
1/4lb broccoli, chopped
1/4lb cauliflower, chopped
3 1/2oz button mushrooms, sliced
14 1/2oz can tomatoes
1 tablespoon chopped fresh parsley
1/2 teaspoon dried mixed herbs
1 cup (1/4lb) grated cheddar cheese
NUTTY CRUMB TOPPING
1 tablespoon butter, melted
3/4 cup fresh whole-wheat bread crumbs
1 cup (5oz) chopped unsalted
   mixed nuts
2 teaspoons chopped fresh parsley

Add rice and bouillon cube to large saucepan of boiling water, boil rapidly, uncovered, about 30 minutes or until tender; drain. Combine rice and egg in medium bowl; mix well. Spread mixture evenly over base of greased ovenproof dish (8 cup capacity).

Melt butter in large skillet, add onion, stir over medium heat about 2 minutes or until onion is soft. Add pepper, broccoli, cauliflower, mushrooms, undrained crushed tomatoes, parsley and herbs, bring to boil. Reduce heat, cover, simmer about 7 minutes or until vegetables are tender. Spoon vegetables evenly over rice.

Sprinkle evenly with cheese, then topping. Bake in 350°F oven 20 minutes.
Nutty Crumb Topping: Combine all ingredients in a small bowl, mix well.

TOFU AND SESAME TARTLETS

Unfilled tartlet cases can be made up to 2 days ahead; keep in airtight container, or freeze for up to 2 months. Fill cases just before serving. Filling suitable to microwave.

PASTRY
2/3 cup whole-wheat flour
1/3 cup all purpose flour
1/4 cup (1/2 stick) butter
1/4 cup sesame seeds
1 egg yolk
1 tablespoon water, approximately
FILLING
10oz packet firm tofu
2 tablespoons (1/4 stick) butter
2 medium onions, sliced
2 stalks celery, chopped
1 small red bell pepper, chopped
1 teaspoon cornstarch
1/3 cup water
2 teaspoons seeded mustard
1/4 large vegetable bouillon
   cube, crumbled
1 tablespoon chopped fresh parsley

Pastry: Grease 4 x 3½ inch flan pans. Sift flours into medium bowl, rub in butter, stir in seeds. Add egg yolk and enough water to mix to a firm dough. Turn pastry onto lightly floured surface, knead lightly until smooth. Cover, refrigerate 30 minutes. Divide pastry into 4 portions. Roll portions large enough to line prepared pans.

Cover each pastry case with baking paper, fill with dried beans or rice. Bake in 375°F oven 7 minutes, remove beans and paper, bake further 7 minutes or until pastry is lightly browned, cool. Remove pastry cases from pans, fill pastry cases with tofu and vegetable filling.

Filling: Place tofu in medium bowl, cover with water, stand 15 minutes, drain. Cut into ¾ inch cubes. Melt butter in medium saucepan, add onions, stir over medium heat about 3 minutes or until onions are soft. Add celery and pepper, stir over medium heat 1 minute.

Blend cornstarch with water, add mustard and bouillon cube, stir into onion mixture, stir over high heat until mixture boils and thickens. Add tofu and parsley, stir gently over heat until heated through.

Makes 4.

ASPARAGUS TIMBALES

Serve timbales hot or cold; they are best made just before serving. Recipe unsuitable to freeze or microwave.

1lb fresh asparagus spears, chopped
2 tablespoons (¼ stick) butter
1 medium onion, chopped
3 tablespoons whole-wheat flour
1 cup (¼lb) grated cheddar cheese
1 egg, lightly beaten
½ large vegetable bouillon
    cube, crumbled
pinch ground nutmeg

Boil, steam or microwave asparagus until tender; drain. Melt butter in small skillet, add onion, stir over medium heat about 2 minutes or until onion is soft. Stir in flour, stir over medium heat 1 minute, transfer to large bowl.

Blend or process asparagus until smooth; add to bowl with cheese, eggs, bouillon cube and nutmeg, mix well. Pour mixture into 6 greased timbale molds (½ cup capacity), cover each mold with foil. Place molds in roasting pan, pour in enough boiling water to come half way up sides of molds. Bake in 325°F oven about 45 minutes or until set. Turn onto plates before serving.

Makes 6.

HERBED TOMATOES WITH CRACKED WHEAT

Filling can be made up to a day ahead; keep, covered, in refrigerator. Recipe unsuitable to freeze or microwave.

¼ cup pine nuts
½ cup cracked wheat
1 medium zucchini, grated
1 tablespoon chopped fresh mint
1 tablespoon chopped fresh oregano
2 green onions, chopped
2 tablespoons fresh lemon juice
2 tablespoons light olive oil
8 medium tomatoes

Toast nuts on baking sheet in 350°F oven about 5 minutes, cool. Place wheat in small bowl, cover with boiling water, stand 15 minutes. Drain in fine strainer, rinse well under cold water, dry as much as possible using absorbent paper.

Place wheat in medium bowl, stir in nuts, zucchini, mint, oregano, onions, juice and oil. Cut bases from tomatoes, reserve for lids, scoop out flesh. Chop flesh, add to wheat mixture. Spoon mixture into tomatoes, replace lids.

Serves 4.

MARINATED BEAN SPROUT AND SESAME SALAD

Recipe can be made 2 hours ahead; keep, covered, in refrigerator. Recipe unsuitable to freeze.

¼ cup sesame seeds
1lb bean sprouts
1 medium red bell pepper, sliced
1 medium green bell pepper, sliced
DRESSING
3 tablespoons olive oil
¼ cup fresh lemon juice
3 tablespoons cider vinegar
2 teaspoons light soy sauce

Stir seeds over heat in small skillet until lightly browned. Combine seeds, sprouts and peppers in large bowl, pour over dressing; toss well, cover, refrigerate about 2 hours, tossing occasionally.
Dressing: Combine all ingredients in a jar, shake well.

Serves 4.

SPICY VEGETABLES IN CRISPY BASKETS

Baskets can be made a day ahead; keep in airtight container. Assemble recipe just before serving. Recipe unsuitable to freeze or microwave.

4 sheets phyllo pastry
¼ cup vegetable oil
SPICY VEGETABLES
1 tablespoon vegetable oil
1 small onion, sliced
1 clove garlic, minced
1 small fresh red chili pepper, chopped
1 medium red bell pepper, chopped
1 medium carrot, sliced
¾lb broccoli, chopped
¼lb snow peas
2 teaspoons light soy sauce
3 tablespoons chopped fresh chives
½ cup water
2 teaspoons cornstarch
1 tablespoon water, extra

Oil the outside of 4 ovenproof dishes (1 cup capacity). Place the dishes upside-down onto lightly greased baking sheet. Cut pastry sheets in half crossways, place 2 sheets on bench. Cover remaining pastry with baking paper, then a damp cloth to prevent drying out. Brush 1 sheet of pastry with oil, top with another sheet of pastry, brush with oil, place over a prepared dish, trim edges. Repeat with remaining pastry. Bake in 350°F oven about 5 minutes or until lightly browned; cool. Carefully remove pastry cases from dishes. Fill cases with vegetables.
Spicy Vegetables: Heat oil in wok or skillet, add onion, garlic and chili, stir-fry 1 minute, or until onion is soft. Add pepper, carrot, broccoli and snow peas, stir-fry 1 minute. Add sauce, chives and water, stir-fry 2 minutes. Blend cornstarch with extra water, add to wok, stir until mixture boils and thickens slightly.

Serves 4.

CARROT, AVOCADO AND SPROUT SALAD

Salad without avocado can be prepared several hours ahead; keep, covered, in refrigerator. Add avocado and dressing just before serving. Recipe unsuitable to freeze.

2½ cups (5oz) bean sprouts
2 medium carrots, grated
1 tablespoon sunflower seed kernels
3 tablespoons chopped fresh parsley
1 medium avocado, sliced

HONEY DRESSING
3 tablespoons olive oil
3 tablespoons fresh lemon juice
2 tablespoons honey
1 clove garlic, minced

Combine sprouts, carrots, kernels and parsley in medium bowl. Pour over dressing, toss well; top with avocado.
Honey Dressing: Combine all ingredients in jar; shake well.
Serves 4.

CHICORY AND PAPAYA SALAD

Salad is best prepared close to serving time. Recipe unsuitable to freeze.

5 cups (½ bunch) chopped chicory
1 small papaya, chopped
4 green onions, chopped
1 large avocado, chopped

DRESSING
¼ cup olive oil
¼ cup fresh lime juice
1 tablespoon grated fresh gingerroot
¼ teaspoon curry powder

Combine chicory, papaya, onions and avocado in large bowl. Add dressing, toss gently to combine.
Dressing: Combine all ingredients in jar, shake well.
Serves 4.

ZUCCHINI AND FETA CHEESE SOUFFLES

Souffles must be made just before serving. This recipe is not suitable to freeze or microwave. Souffle mixture suitable to microwave.

1 medium zucchini, grated
salt
3 tablespoons butter
¼ cup all-purpose flour
¼ teaspoon dry mustard
1 cup milk
¼lb feta cheese, crumbled
2 tablespoons grated
    Parmesan cheese
4 eggs, separated

Place zucchini into colander, sprinkle with salt; toss lightly, stand over a bowl for 30 minutes to drain. Rinse zucchini under cold water, drain, squeeze out excess liquid from zucchini.

Melt butter in medium saucepan, stir in flour and mustard, stir over medium heat 1 minute. Remove from heat, gradually stir in milk, stir over high heat until mixture bolls and thickens; remove from heat, transfer to large bowl, stir in cheeses, zucchini and egg yolks.

Beat egg whites in medium bowl until soft peaks form, fold into zucchini mixture in 2 batches. Pour mixture into 4 ovenproof dishes (1 cup capacity). Place dishes on baking sheet, bake in 350°F oven about 25 minutes or until souffles are golden brown.

Serves 4.

LEFT: From left: Carrot, Avocado and Sprout Salad; Chicory and Papaya Salad.
ABOVE: Spicy Vegetables in Crispy Baskets.

BUCKWHEAT CREPES WITH SPICY GREEN BEAN FILLING

Unfilled crepes can be made 2 days ahead; keep, layered with baking paper, in refrigerator. Crepes can be frozen for 2 months. Filling is best prepared close to serving time. Recipe unsuitable to microwave.

BUCKWHEAT CREPES
½ cup whole-wheat flour
½ cup buckwheat flour
1 egg, lightly beaten
1½ cups milk
1 tablespoon butter
3½oz oyster mushrooms

SPICY GREEN BEAN FILLING
10oz green beans
2 teaspoons vegetable oil
1 medium onion, chopped
2 cloves garlic, minced
1 small red bell pepper, chopped
2 teaspoons garam masala
2 teaspoons ground cumin
½ teaspoon ground turmeric

¼ teaspoon chili powder
5 medium tomatoes, peeled
2 tablespoons tomato paste
½ cup canned drained whole-kernel corn
½ cup plain yogurt

Buckwheat Crepes: Sift flours into medium bowl, make well in center, gradually stir in combined egg and milk, mix to a smooth batter (or, blend or process all ingredients until smooth). Cover, stand 30 minutes.

Pour 3 to 4 tablespoons of batter into heated greased heavy-based small crepe pan; cook until lightly browned underneath. Turn crepe, brown on other side. Repeat with remaining batter. You will need 12 crepes. Divide filling between crepes, fold crepes into quarters.

Melt butter in small skillet, add mushrooms, stir over medium heat about 3 minutes or until tender. Serve with crepes.

Spicy Green Bean Filling: Cut beans lengthways into strips, then cut in half. Boil, steam or microwave until tender.

Heat oil in medium saucepan, add onion, garlic and pepper, stir over medium heat about 2 minutes or until onion is soft.

Add spices, tomatoes, paste and corn, bring to boil, reduce heat, cover, simmer 10 minutes. Add beans, stir until heated through. Remove from heat, gradually stir in yogurt.

Serves 6.

BELOW: Buckwheat Crepes with Spicy Green Bean Filling.
LEFT: Zucchini and Feta Cheese Souffles.

CORNMEAL AND HERB SEASONED ARTICHOKES

Artichokes can be prepared several hours ahead; keep, covered, in refrigerator. Recipe unsuitable to freeze or microwave.

4 medium artichokes
2 teaspoons vegetable oil
2 stalks celery, chopped
3 tablespoons chopped fresh chives
3 tablespoons chopped fresh sage
²⁄₃ cup fresh whole-wheat bread crumbs
¹⁄₃ cup yellow cornmeal
¹⁄₂ cup roasted unsalted cashew nuts, chopped
1 egg, lightly beaten
¹⁄₄ cup fresh lemon juice

LEMON SAGE SAUCE
1 cup water
¹⁄₃ cup fresh lemon juice
1 tablespoon chopped fresh sage
1 tablespoon light soy sauce
1 tablespoon cornstarch
2 tablespoons water, extra

Cut bases from artichokes so they sit flat. Remove tough outer leaves, and shorten the remaining leaves with scissors.

Heat oil in small skillet, add celery, chives and sage, stir over medium heat until celery is soft; stir in bread crumbs, cornmeal and nuts, stir over heat further minute. Remove from heat; cool. Stir in egg; mix well.

Starting from outside of each artichoke, press seasoning between leaves until artichokes are packed tightly. Place in single layer in roasting pan, pour over lemon juice, bake, uncovered, in 350°F oven about 40 minutes or until artichokes are tender; brush occasionally with juice during cooking. Serve topped with sauce.
Lemon Sage Sauce: Combine water, juice, sage and sauce in small saucepan, bring to boil, reduce heat, simmer, uncovered, 5 minutes.

Blend cornstarch with extra water, add to pan, stir over high heat until sauce boils and thickens.

Serves 4.

BELOW: Cornmeal and Herb Seasoned Artichokes.

MainCourses

Meals to remember are built around dishes
like these. We dressed vegetables with
flair and made them more tempting
than ever before. And we used nuts, beans,
pastry, pasta, cheese and more in lots
of healthy, tasty ways you will enjoy.
Some can also be served as appetizers.
If you like: others would make
delicious party fare.

HONEYED CABBAGE AND PINEAPPLE STIR-FRY

Stir-fry is best made close to serving
time. This recipe is not suitable to
freeze. Potato suitable to microwave.

1 large sweet potato
1 tablespoon vegetable oil
1 medium onion, quartered
½ small cabbage, shredded
4 cups (10oz) bean sprouts
1 medium red bell pepper, sliced
14½oz can unsweetened pineapple
   chunks, drained
1 tablespoon hoisin sauce
1 tablespoon light soy sauce
1 tablespoon honey

Cut sweet potato into 2 inch sticks; boil,
steam or microwave until just tender.

Heat oil in large skillet or wok, add
onion, stir-fry about 2 minutes or until
onion is soft. Add cabbage, sprouts and
pepper, stir-fry further 2 minutes. Stir in
pineapple with combined sauces and
honey. Stir-fry further minute.

Serves 4.

ABOVE: Honeyed Cabbage and Pineapple Stir-Fry.

PUMPKIN PASTA WITH FRESH VEGETABLE SAUCE

You will need to cook about 7oz pumpkin squash for this recipe. Recipe is best prepared just before serving. Pasta can be frozen for 2 months. Sauce unsuitable to freeze or microwave.

PUMPKIN PASTA
1¾ cups all-purpose flour
2 eggs
**½ cup cold, mashed, cooked
    pumpkin squash**

FRESH VEGETABLE SAUCE
1 medium carrot
2 medium zucchini
2 tablespoons vegetable oil
1 medium onion, chopped
1 medium red bell pepper, sliced
1 tablespoon whole-wheat flour
2 medium tomatoes, peeled, chopped
1 teaspoon chopped fresh marjoram
1 teaspoon chopped fresh basil
2 teaspoons tomato paste
1 teaspoon dark brown sugar
1 cup water
**½ large vegetable bouillon
    cube, crumbled**

Pumpkin Pasta: Process flour, eggs and squash until mixture is well combined and forms a ball. Turn dough onto lightly floured surface, knead for 5 minutes. Wrap dough in plastic wrap, refrigerate 30 minutes. Divide dough into 4 portions. Place 1 portion on bench, cover remaining dough with plastic wrap to prevent drying out.

Roll dough on lightly floured surface to a rectangle ¹⁄₁₆ inch thick, sprinkle lightly with flour, roll up firmly from a narrow end. Cut dough into ¼ inch slices, unroll strips, place onto tray to dry about 15 minutes. Repeat with remaining dough. Add pasta gradually to large saucepan of boiling water, boil, uncovered, 4 minutes; drain. Serve pasta with sauce.

Fresh Vegetable Sauce: Cut carrot and zucchini into thin strips. Heat oil in large skillet, add onion and carrot, stir over medium heat about 3 minutes or until onion is soft. Add zucchini and pepper, stir over medium heat 3 minutes. Stir in flour, stir over medium heat further minute.

Stir in tomatoes, marjoram, basil, paste, sugar, water and bouillon cube, stir over high heat until mixture boils and thickens slightly, cover, reduce heat, simmer about 7 minutes or until vegetables are tender.

Serves 4.

RIGHT: From top: Pumpkin Pasta with Fresh Vegetable Sauce; Whole-Wheat Ravioli with Eggplant Filling.

WHOLE-WHEAT RAVIOLI WITH EGGPLANT FILLING

Ravioli can be made 2 days ahead; keep, covered, in refrigerator or freeze for up to 2 months. Ravioli dough can be rolled using a pasta machine; follow manufacturer's directions. Recipe unsuitable to microwave.

RAVIOLI
2 cups whole-wheat flour
2 eggs, lightly beaten
2 tablespoons vegetable oil
1/3 cup water
3 tablespoons chopped fresh parsley
1/2 cup grated Parmesan cheese

EGGPLANT FILLING
1 medium eggplant, chopped
1 medium zucchini, chopped
salt
2 tablespoons (1/4 stick) butter
1 medium onion, chopped
3 1/2 oz ricotta cheese
1 egg, lightly beaten
2 tablespoons chopped fresh parsley

STEP 1

Ravioli: Process flour, eggs, oil and water until mixture forms a ball.

STEP 2

Turn dough onto lightly floured surface, knead 5 minutes. Wrap dough in plastic wrap, refrigerate 30 minutes. Divide dough into 4 portions. Place 1 portion on bench, cover remaining dough with plastic wrap to prevent drying out. Roll dough out to 1/16 inch thickness on lightly floured surface, cut into 2 x 6 inch strips.

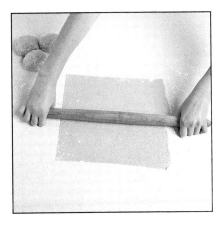

STEP 3

Cover 1 dough strip with tea-towel to prevent drying out. Place heaped teaspoons of filling at 3/4 inch intervals on 1 strip of dough.

STEP 4

Lightly brush edges and between mounds of filling with water, top with a second dough strip, press edges together to seal.

STEP 5

Cut between mounds of filling using knife or fluted pastry cutter. Repeat with remaining dough and filling. Add ravioli gradually to large saucepan of boiling water, boil, uncovered, about 8 minutes or until tender; drain. Serve sprinkled with parsley and Parmesan cheese.

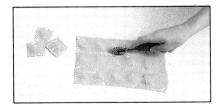

Eggplant Filling: Place eggplant and zucchini in colander, sprinkle with salt, stand 30 minutes, rinse under cold water; drain. Melt butter in large skillet, add onion, stir over medium heat about 3 minutes or until onion is soft. Add eggplant and zucchini, stir over medium heat about 5 minutes or until eggplant is soft; cool to room temperature. Blend or process eggplant mixture until smooth, transfer mixture to medium bowl. Add ricotta cheese, egg and parsley, stir well.

Serves 4.

LETTUCE ROLLS WITH BEET SALAD

Make rolls close to serving time. Salad can be made a day ahead. Recipe unsuitable to freeze. Suitable to microwave.

1 medium carrot, chopped
7oz yellow pattypan squash, chopped
½ cup fresh or frozen peas
1 medium cucumber, chopped
1 medium tomato, chopped
6 green onions, chopped
¼ cup plain yogurt
2 teaspoons tamari shoyu
¼ teaspoon Oriental sesame oil
1 teaspoon grated lemon zest
1 clove garlic, minced
1 tablespoon chopped fresh mint
12 large lettuce leaves

BEET SALAD
4 medium beets
1 tablespoon olive oil
1 tablespoon raspberry vinegar
1 tablespoon chopped fresh parsley

Boil, steam or microwave carrot, squash and peas until tender; place in large bowl. Add cucumber, tomato and onions with combined yogurt, tamari shoyu, oil, zest, garlic and mint; mix well. Drop lettuce leaves into large saucepan of boiling water, drain immediately. Place leaves into a bowl of iced water, drain on absorbent paper. Spoon filling evenly onto center of each leaf, wrap securely. Serve rolls with beet salad.

Beet Salad: Cover beets with water in large saucepan, bring to boil, reduce heat, cover, simmer about 30 minutes or until tender, drain; cool. Peel beets, slice thickly. Place into medium bowl, add combined oil, vinegar and parsley.

Serves 4.

CAULIFLOWER AND CELERY PIES

Filling can be made a day ahead; keep, covered, in refrigerator. Recipe unsuitable to freeze. Filling suitable to microwave.

PASTRY
1 cup whole-wheat flour
¼ cup oat bran
3oz (¾ stick) butter
2 tablespoons water, approximately
1 egg, lightly beaten
2 tablespoons sesame seeds

FILLING
½ small cauliflower, chopped
2 tablespoons (¼ stick) butter
1 medium onion, thinly sliced
2 stalks celery, thinly sliced
¼ cup all-purpose flour
2¼ cups water
1 large vegetable bouillon
   cube, crumbled
1 tablespoon seeded mustard

Pastry: Combine flour and oat bran in medium bowl, rub in butter. Add enough water to mix to a firm dough (pastry can also be made in food processor). Cover, refrigerate 30 minutes. Roll pastry between 2 sheets of plastic wrap or baking paper until about ¼ inch thick.

Spoon filling into 6 ovenproof dishes (¾ cup capacity), brush edges of dishes with egg. Cut pastry into 6 rounds large enough to cover dishes, place on dishes, press firmly around edges then decorate with fork, if desired. Brush pastry with remaining egg, sprinkle with sesame seeds. Bake in 375°F oven about 20 minutes or until pastry is well browned.

Filling: Boil, steam or microwave cauliflower until just tender, drain.

Melt butter in large saucepan, add onion and celery, stir over medium heat about 2 minutes or until onion is soft. Stir in flour, stir over medium heat further minute. Remove from heat, gradually stir in combined water, bouillon cube and mustard, stir over high heat until mixture boils and thickens; add cauliflower.

Serves 6.

*BELOW: Cauliflower and Celery Pies.
LEFT: Lettuce Rolls with Beet Salad*

CHEESY NUT LOAF WITH TOMATO SAUCE

Loaf and sauce can be made a day ahead; keep, covered, in refrigerator. You will need to cook ½ cup brown rice for this recipe. This recipe is unsuitable to freeze. Sauce suitable to microwave.

1 tablespoon olive oil
1 medium onion, chopped
1 medium green bell pepper, chopped
1 medium tomato, chopped
1 cup (5oz) roasted unsalted
　cashew nuts
1 cup (5½oz) blanched almonds
1 medium carrot, grated
1 cup cooked brown rice
¾ cup grated cheddar cheese
1 egg, lightly beaten

TOMATO SAUCE
1 tablespoon olive oil
6 medium tomatoes, chopped
¼ cup water

Lightly oil 5½ inch x 8 inch loaf pan, line base with baking paper. Heat oil in saucepan, add onion, pepper and tomato, stir over heat about 4 minutes or until pepper is tender; cool. Blend or process cashews and almonds until finely chopped.

Combine onion mixture, nuts, carrot, rice, cheese and egg in a large bowl, mix well. Press mixture evenly into prepared pan, bake in 350°F oven about 40 minutes or until lightly browned. Serve with sauce.

Tomato Sauce: Heat oil in medium saucepan, add tomatoes, cook over low heat 10 minutes. Blend or process tomatoes and water until smooth, strain; reheat before serving.

Serves 4.

SPINACH AND MUSHROOM TIMBALES

Cook timbales close to serving time. This recipe is not suitable to freeze. Spinach and mushroom layer mixtures and sauce suitable to microwave.

SPINACH LAYER
1 bunch (20oz) spinach
1 egg
pinch nutmeg
2 tablespoons milk

MUSHROOM LAYER
2 tablespoons (¼ stick) butter
1 clove garlic, minced
1 medium onion, finely chopped
½lb mushrooms, sliced
2 tablespoons whole-wheat flour
½ cup milk
2 eggs, lightly beaten

GARLIC AND CHIVE SAUCE
2 teaspoons butter
1 clove garlic, minced
1½ teaspoons all-purpose flour
½ cup milk
2 tablespoons chopped fresh chives

Lightly grease 4 ovenproof dishes (¾ cup capacity). Spoon spinach layer evenly into dishes, top with mushroom layer; cover dishes with foil. Place dishes in roasting pan, pour in enough boiling water to come halfway up sides of dishes. Bake in 350°F oven about 1 hour or until set. Stand 5 minutes before turning onto serving plates. Serve with sauce.

Spinach Layer: Boil, steam or microwave spinach until tender; drain well. Blend spinach, egg, nutmeg and milk until smooth.

Mushroom Layer: Melt butter in medium saucepan, add garlic and onion, stir over medium heat about 2 minutes or until onion is soft.

Add mushrooms, stir over medium heat 2 minutes. Stir in flour, stir over medium heat 1 minute. Remove from heat, gradually stir in milk, stir over high heat until mixture boils and thickens. Cool slightly 5 minutes; stir in eggs.

Garlic and Chive Sauce: Melt butter with garlic in small saucepan. Stir in flour, stir over medium heat 30 seconds. Remove from heat, gradually stir in milk, stir over high heat until mixture boils and thickens. Strain sauce, stir in chives.

Serves 4.

BRAZIL NUT CUTLETS WITH PIMIENTO SAUCE

Cutlets can be made a day ahead; keep, covered, in refrigerator. Cooked cutlets and sauce can be frozen for up to a month. Sauce suitable to microwave.

2 cups (10oz) Brazil nuts, finely chopped
1 cup (2½oz) fresh whole-wheat bread crumbs
3 tablespoons chopped fresh parsley
2 eggs, lightly beaten
2 tablespoons olive oil

PIMIENTO SAUCE
7oz can pimientos, drained
1 large vegetable bouillon cube, crumbled
¼ cup water
¼ cup chopped fresh parsley

Combine nuts, bread crumbs, parsley and eggs in medium bowl; mix well. Divide mixture into 8 portions, shape into cutlets or patties; refrigerate 30 minutes. Heat oil in large skillet, add cutlets, cook over medium heat 2 minutes on each side or until golden brown. Serve with sauce.

Pimiento Sauce: Blend or process pimientos, bouillon cube and water until smooth; pour into small saucepan. Stir over medium heat about 2 minutes. Stir in parsley before serving.

Makes 8.

ABOVE: From left: Brazil Nut Cutlets with Pimiento Sauce; Cheesy Nut Loaf with Tomato Sauce.
LEFT: Spinach and Mushroom Timbales.

CARROT PARCELS WITH BASIL SAUCE

You will need to grate about 4 medium carrots for this recipe. Recipe unsuitable to freeze or microwave.

2 tablespoons (¼ stick) butter
1 small leek, sliced
3 cups grated carrot
½lb ricotta cheese
3 tablespoons chopped fresh parsley
3 tablespoons sunflower seed kernels
1 egg, lightly beaten
6 sheets phyllo pastry
3 tablespoons butter, melted, extra
1 tablespoon packaged unseasoned
    bread crumbs

BASIL SAUCE
1 tablespoon butter
1 clove garlic, minced
1 tablespoon whole-wheat flour
⅔ cup milk
½ cup heavy cream
2 tablespoons chopped fresh basil
1 tablespoon grated
    Parmesan cheese

Melt butter in small saucepan, add leek, stir over medium heat about 3 minutes or until soft. Combine leek, carrot, cheese, parsley, kernels and egg in large bowl.

Cut pastry sheets in half crossways, place 3 pastry sheets on bench, cover remaining pastry with baking paper, then a damp cloth to prevent drying out. Layer the 3 pastry sheets together, brushing each sheet with the extra butter.

Place quarter of the carrot mixture along short end of pastry, fold in sides and roll up like a jelly-roll. Repeat with remaining pastry, extra butter and carrot mixture.

Place parcels on greased baking sheet, brush with extra butter, sprinkle with bread crumbs. Bake in 350°F oven about 30 minutes or until golden brown. Serve with basil sauce.

Basil Sauce: Melt butter with garlic in medium saucepan. Stir in flour, stir over medium heat 1 minute. Remove from heat, gradually stir in combined milk and cream, stir over high heat until mixture boils and thickens. Remove from heat, stir in basil and cheese.

Makes 4.

CHILI VEGETABLE HOT POT

Recipe can be prepared 3 hours ahead; keep, covered, in refrigerator. This recipe is not suitable to freeze or microwave.

2 tablespoons olive oil
1 clove garlic, minced
1 small fresh red chili
    pepper, chopped
2 medium red onions, chopped
2 medium carrots, chopped
2 medium red bell peppers, chopped
14½oz can tomatoes
½ cup water
1 tablespoon tomato paste
½ teaspoon ground cumin
8oz can red kidney beans, drained
3oz mushrooms, sliced
3 tablespoons chopped fresh parsley

Heat oil in medium skillet, add garlic, chili and onions, stir occasionally over low heat about 15 minutes or until onions are soft. Add carrots and peppers, stir 1 minute. Add undrained crushed tomatoes, water, paste and cumin, bring to boil, reduce heat, cover, simmer about 10 minutes. Add beans and mushrooms, simmer 5 minutes. Sprinkle hot pot with parsley just before serving.

Serves 4.

BELOW: Carrot Parcels with Basil Sauce.
RIGHT: From top: Chili Vegetable Hot Pot;
Potato Crusted Lentil Hot Pot.

BLACK-EYED BEAN CASSEROLE

Casserole can be made up to a day ahead; keep, covered, in refrigerator. This recipe is not suitable to freeze or microwave.

1½ cups (½lb) black-eyed beans
14½oz can tomatoes
1 medium red onion, chopped
1 clove garlic, minced
½ cup tomato paste
1 small green bell pepper, chopped
3 cups water
¼ cup chopped fresh parsley
¼ cup chopped fresh basil
1lb button mushrooms, sliced
11oz can whole-kernel corn, drained

Cover beans with cold water, stand overnight. Drain beans, place in medium saucepan with enough water to cover, bring to boil, boil 30 minutes, drain.

Combine beans, undrained crushed tomatoes, onion, garlic, paste, pepper and water in a large saucepan. Bring to boil, reduce heat, cover, simmer 1 hour, stirring occasionally, or until beans are tender. Add parsley, basil, mushrooms and corn, simmer further 15 minutes.

Serves 4 to 6.

PEANUT PATTIES WITH SPICY BARBEQUE SAUCE

Peanut mixture can be made several hours ahead; keep, covered, in refrigerator. You will need to cook about ¾ cup brown rice for this recipe. This recipe is not suitable to freeze or microwave.

1¼ cups (5oz) unsalted
    roasted peanuts
1½ cups cooked brown rice
1 medium onion, chopped
2 eggs
3 tablespoons smooth peanut butter
2 tablespoons fruit chutney
1½ teaspoons curry powder
2 tablespoons vegetable oil

SPICY BARBEQUE SAUCE
2 teaspoons cornstarch
½ cup water
½ cup tomato ketchup
2 teaspoons Worcestershire sauce
½ teaspoon tabasco sauce
1 tablespoon dark brown sugar

Blend or process peanuts and rice until finely chopped, add onion, eggs, peanut butter, chutney and curry powder; process until combined. Refrigerate mixture at least 30 minutes.

Using lightly floured hands, shape mixture into 8 patties. Heat oil in large skillet, add patties, cook about 5 minutes or until browned on both sides; drain on absorbent paper. Serve patties with spicy barbeque sauce.

Spicy Barbeque Sauce: Blend cornstarch with water in small saucepan, add remaining ingredients, stir over high heat until mixture boils and thickens.

Makes 8.

POLENTA AND EGGPLANT WITH TOMATO SAUCE

Polenta and sauce can be made up to a day ahead; keep, covered, in refrigerator. Polenta and eggplant unsuitable to freeze. Sauce can be frozen up to 2 months. Sauce suitable to microwave.

4 cups water
1 cup (7oz) yellow cornmeal
¼ cup olive oil
1 medium eggplant
salt
all-purpose flour
oil for shallow-frying, extra

TOMATO SAUCE
2 teaspoons olive oil
1 medium red bell pepper, chopped
1 medium onion, chopped
1 clove garlic, minced
1 teaspoon dried oregano leaves
14½oz can tomatoes
3 tablespoons tomato paste
¼ cup water

Lightly oil 7½ inch x 11½ inch baking pan. Place water into large saucepan, bring to boil. Gradually sprinkle cornmeal into water; mix well. Cover, reduce heat to low; cook, stirring occasionally, about 30 minutes or until polenta is very thick. Spread mixture evenly into prepared pan, cool; stand 2 hours. Cut polenta into 12 pieces. Heat oil in a large skillet, add polenta, cook about 3 minutes each side or until golden; keep warm.

Cut eggplant into ½ inch strips, place in colander, sprinkle with salt; stand 30 minutes. Rinse eggplant under cold water, drain, pat dry with absorbent paper. Toss eggplant strips in flour; shake away excess flour. Shallow-fry strips in batches in hot extra oil until golden brown; drain on absorbent paper; keep warm.

Pour smooth sauce evenly into pasta plates, top with polenta and eggplant, top with remaining sauce.

Tomato Sauce: Heat oil in large saucepan, add pepper, onion, garlic and oregano, stir over medium heat about 2 minutes or until onion is soft. Add undrained crushed tomatoes, tomato paste and water, cook over medium heat about 20 minutes or until vegetables are soft. Blend or process half the sauce mixture until smooth.

Serves 4.

BELOW: From left: Vegetable Rissoles with Plum Sauce; Polenta and Eggplant with Tomato Sauce.
LEFT: From left: Black-Eyed Bean Casserole; Peanut Patties with Spicy Barbeque Sauce.

51

VEGETABLE RISSOLES WITH PLUM SAUCE

Recipe can be made up to 3 days ahead; keep, covered, in refrigerator. This recipe is not suitable to freeze or microwave.

½ cup red lentils
1½ cups water
15oz can garbanzo beans, drained
1 tablespoon olive oil
1 medium leek, finely sliced
1 medium carrot, grated
½ teaspoon ground cumin
½ teaspoon ground coriander
2 tablespoons chopped fresh mint
2 teaspoons fresh lemon juice
¼ cup packaged unseasoned
    bread crumbs
¼ cup packaged unseasoned
    bread crumbs, extra
¼ cup sliced almonds, crushed
1 tablespoon olive oil, extra

PLUM SAUCE
1 teaspoon olive oil
1 medium onion, sliced
14oz can dessert plums
2 tablespoons light soy sauce
1 tablespoon superfine sugar
1 teaspoon cornstarch
¼ cup water

Place lentils and water in medium saucepan, bring to boil, reduce heat, cover, simmer about 10 minutes or until lentils are soft, drain. Blend or process garbanzo beans until smooth.

Heat oil in large saucepan, add leek and carrot, stir over medium heat about 3 minutes or until leek is soft. Add cumin, coriander, mint, juice and bread crumbs. Add lentils and garbanzo beans to pan, mix well; cool.

Divide mixture into 8 portions, shape into rissoles, toss in combined extra bread crumbs and almonds. Heat extra oil in large skillet, add rissoles, cook over medium heat about 5 minutes on each side or until golden brown. Serve with plum sauce.

Plum Sauce: Heat oil in small saucepan, add onion, cook over low heat about 5 minutes or until soft. Drain plums, reserve ¼ cup of the syrup. Blend or process plums, reserved syrup, sauce and sugar until smooth, return to pan. Blend cornstarch with water, add to mixture in pan, stir over high heat until mixture boils and thickens slightly.

Serves 4.

RIGHT: From top: Minted Sprout and Tempeh Salad; Fresh Herb Seasoned Eggs.
FAR RIGHT: Vegetable Parcels with Yogurt Sauce.

52

MINTED SPROUT AND TEMPEH SALAD

Salad and dressing can be made several hours ahead; keep, covered, in refrigerator. Recipe unsuitable to freeze or microwave.

2 tablespoons sesame seeds
½ x 10oz package tempeh, sliced
¼ cup cider vinegar
1 tablespoon grated fresh gingerroot
¼ cup tamari shoyu
whole-wheat flour
1 egg, lightly beaten
¼ cup skim milk
1 cup (2½oz) fresh whole-wheat bread crumbs
1 cup (5oz) finely chopped unsalted raw peanuts
oil for shallow-frying
1 medium honeydew melon, chopped
1 medium green cucumber, chopped
4 green onions, chopped
2 medium oranges
1 cup (2½oz) bean sprouts
DRESSING
1 cup plain yogurt
3 tablespoons smooth peanut butter
2 tablespoons chopped fresh mint
1 tablespoon tamari shoyu
1 tablespoon fresh lemon juice
1 tablespoon honey

Stir seeds over heat in small skillet until lightly browned, remove from skillet.

Combine tempeh, vinegar, gingerroot and tamari shoyu in small bowl, cover, refrigerate overnight.

Remove tempeh from marinade; drain on absorbent paper. Dust with flour, dip into combined egg and milk, then into combined bread crumbs and peanuts. Shallow-fry tempeh in hot oil until golden brown; drain tempeh on absorbent paper.

Combine tempeh, melon, cucumber, onions, orange segments and sprouts in a large bowl. Pour over dressing, sprinkle with sesame seeds just before serving.
Dressing: Combine all ingredients in small bowl; mix well.

Serves 4.

FRESH HERB SEASONED EGGS

Eggs can be hard-boiled a day ahead; keep, covered, in refrigerator. Seasoning is best prepared close to serving time. Recipe unsuitable to freeze or microwave.

8 hard-boiled eggs
8 cherry tomatoes, halved
1½ cups (2½oz) watercress sprigs
FRESH HERB SEASONING
¼ cup mayonnaise
2 tablespoons chopped fresh parsley
1 tablespoon chopped fresh chives
1 teaspoon chopped fresh thyme
3 tablespoons grated Parmesan cheese

Cut eggs in half crossways, reserve yolks for seasoning. Place seasoning into piping bag fitted with large fluted tube, pipe mixture into egg halves. Serve with tomatoes and watercress.
Fresh Herb Seasoning: Push reserved yolks through fine strainer into medium bowl, stir in remaining ingredients.

Serves 4.

VEGETABLE PARCELS WITH YOGURT SAUCE

Parcels can be prepared a day ahead; keep, covered, in refrigerator. Recipe unsuitable to freeze or microwave.

⅓ cup vegetable oil
¼ teaspoon black mustard seeds
1 tablespoon finely chopped fresh gingerroot
1 medium onion, finely chopped
¼ teaspoon ground turmeric
¼ teaspoon chili powder
1 teaspoon ground cumin
2 teaspoons ground coriander
½ teaspoon garam masala
¼ teaspoon Vecon
4 medium carrots, chopped
1 cup (¼lb) frozen peas
½ cup chopped fresh cilantro
¼ cup water
8 sheets phyllo pastry
¼ cup vegetable oil, extra

YOGURT SAUCE
½ cup plain yogurt
¼ cup mango chutney
2 teaspoons chopped fresh cilantro

Heat oil in large saucepan, add seeds, stir over medium heat until seeds begin to pop. Add gingerroot and onion, stir over medium heat about 2 minutes or until onion is soft. Stir in turmeric, chili, cumin, coriander, garam masala and Vecon, cook 1 minute. Add carrots, peas, cilantro and water to pan, cover, cook over low heat about 20 minutes or until vegetables are tender, stirring occasionally; cool.

Brush 1 sheet of pastry with extra oil, top with another sheet of pastry, brush with oil. Place a quarter of mixture along short side of pastry, leaving 2 inch border, fold sides in, roll up like a jelly-roll. Brush all over with more extra oil, place onto baking sheet. Repeat with remaining pastry, oil and filling. Bake in 350°F oven about 30 minutes or until lightly browned. Serve with yogurt sauce.
Yogurt Sauce: Combine all ingredients in small bowl.

Makes 4.

WHOLE-WHEAT SWISS CHARD AND RICOTTA CREPES

Recipe can be prepared several hours ahead; keep, covered, in refrigerator. Bake just before serving. Crepes can be frozen for up to 2 months. Sauce suitable to microwave.

CREPES
½ cup whole-wheat flour
½ cup all-purpose flour
3 eggs, lightly beaten
1¼ cups milk
1 tablespoon butter, melted
1 cup (2½oz) fresh whole-wheat bread crumbs
¼ cup grated Parmesan cheese

SWISS CHARD AND RICOTTA FILLING
2 tablespoons (¼ stick) butter
1 clove garlic, minced
1 bunch Swiss chard, chopped
½lb ricotta cheese
¼ cup grated Parmesan cheese
¼ teaspoon ground cumin

SAUCE
2 tablespoons (¼ stick) butter
2 tablespoons whole-wheat flour
1¼ cups skim milk

Crepes: Sift flours into large bowl, make well in center, gradually stir in combined eggs, milk and butter, mix to a smooth batter (or, blend or process all ingredients until smooth). Cover, stand 30 minutes. Pour 3 to 4 tablespoons of batter into heated greased heavy-based crepe pan, cook until lightly browned underneath. Turn crepe, brown other side. Repeat with remaining batter. You will need 12 crepes for this recipe.

Divide filling evenly between crepes, roll up, place in single layer in lightly greased shallow ovenproof dish, top with sauce, sprinkle with combined bread crumbs and cheese. Bake in 350°F oven about 30 minutes or until well browned.

Swiss Chard and Ricotta Filling: Melt butter in medium skillet, add garlic and Swiss chard, stir over heat until Swiss chard is tender and all liquid has evaporated. Process Swiss chard with remaining ingredients until finely chopped.

Sauce: Melt butter in small saucepan, stir in flour, stir over heat 1 minute. Remove from heat, gradually stir in milk, stir over high heat until mixture boils and thickens.

Serves 6.

RIGHT: From left: Whole-Wheat Swiss Chard and Ricotta Crepes; Vegetable and Tofu Lasagne.

VEGETABLE AND TOFU LASAGNE

Lasagne can be prepared a day ahead; keep, covered, in refrigerator. Lasagne can be frozen for a month. Cooked packaged lasagne can be used; you will need 5oz (9 sheets) of whole-wheat lasagne noodles.

1 tablespoon olive oil
2 medium onions, chopped
2 cloves garlic, minced
2 medium carrots, chopped
2 large stalks celery, chopped
1 medium red bell pepper, chopped
7oz mushrooms, chopped
6 medium tomatoes, peeled, chopped
3 tablespoons tomato paste
¼ cup chopped fresh basil
¼ cup chopped fresh parsley
¾ cup soft tofu
10oz fresh whole-wheat
    lasagne noodles
¼ cup fresh whole-wheat
    bread crumbs
2 tablespoons grated
    Parmesan cheese

Heat oil in large saucepan, add onions, garlic, carrots, celery and pepper, stir over medium heat about 5 minutes or until onions are soft. Add mushrooms, stir over medium heat 1 minute. Stir in tomatoes, tomato paste and herbs, bring to boil, reduce heat, cover, simmer about 15 minutes or until vegetables are tender. Remove from heat.

Beat tofu in small bowl until smooth, add ¼ cup of the tofu to vegetable mixture, mix well.

Cut pasta into 6 rectangles measuring about 4 inches x 10 inches. Spread a third of the vegetable mixture into greased 8 inch x 10 inch ovenproof dish (8 cup capacity). Top with 2 sheets of pasta. Continue layering vegetable mixture and pasta, finishing with a layer of pasta.

Spread remaining tofu evenly over pasta, sprinkle with combined bread crumbs and cheese. Bake in 350°F oven about 50 minutes or until golden brown.

Serves 4.

CREPES WITH CREAMY BROCCOLI FILLING

Crepes can be made a day ahead; keep, covered, in refrigerator, or freeze up to 2 months. Filling unsuitable to freeze; suitable to microwave.

CREPES
⅓ cup whole-wheat flour
3 tablespoons self-rising flour
2 eggs, lightly beaten
⅔ cup milk
1 tablespoon vegetable oil
¼ cup grated Parmesan cheese

CREAMY BROCCOLI FILLING
1½lb broccoli, chopped
2 tablespoons (¼ stick) butter
2 green onions, chopped
1 tablespoon whole-wheat flour
1 large vegetable bouillon cube, crumbled
½ cup milk
½ cup heavy cream
pinch ground nutmeg
1 tablespoon chopped fresh basil

Crepes: Sift flours into large bowl, make well in center, gradually stir in combined eggs, milk and oil, mix to a smooth batter (or, blend or process all ingredients until smooth). Cover, stand 30 minutes. Pour 3 to 4 tablespoons of batter into heated greased heavy-based crepe pan; cook until lightly browned underneath. Turn crepe, brown on other side. Repeat with remaining batter. You will need 8 crepes for this recipe.

Divide filling between crepes, fold crepes into triangles. Place crepes into lightly greased ovenproof dish, sprinkle with cheese, bake in 350˚F oven about 10 minutes or until heated through.

Creamy Broccoli Filling: Boil, steam or microwave broccoli until tender; drain. Melt butter in saucepan, add onions, stir over medium heat 1 minute. Stir in flour, stir over medium heat 1 minute. Remove from heat, gradually stir in combined bouillon cube, milk, cream and nutmeg, stir over high heat until mixture boils and thickens; stir in broccoli and basil.

Serves 4.

LEFT: From left: Pea Souffle Omelets; Crepes with Creamy Broccoli Filling.

PEA SOUFFLE OMELETS

Make omelets just before serving. Sauce can be made a day ahead; keep, covered, in refrigerator. Recipe unsuitable to freeze or microwave.

1 cup (¼lb) fresh or frozen peas
4 eggs, separated
¼ cup grated cheddar cheese

VEGETABLE SAUCE
2 tablespoons (¼ stick) butter
1 small onion, thinly sliced
1 stalk celery, thinly sliced
1 small carrot, thinly sliced
1 tablespoon whole-wheat flour
1¼ cups water
3 tablespoons sour cream
1 tablespoon chopped fresh mint

Boil, steam or microwave peas until tender; drain. Blend or process peas until smooth; push through sieve.

Beat egg yolks in large bowl until thick, stir in pea puree. Beat egg whites in medium bowl until soft peaks form, gently fold into pea mixture. Pour half the mixture into heated greased small skillet, cook over high heat until browned underneath, place skillet under hot broiler until surface of omelet is set.

Sprinkle omelet with cheese, fold in half, place on serving plate; serve immediately. Repeat with remaining mixture. Serve omelets with vegetable sauce.

Vegetable Sauce: Melt butter in medium saucepan, add onion, celery and carrot, stir over medium heat about 3 minutes or until carrot is soft. Stir in flour, stir over medium heat 1 minute. Remove from heat, gradually stir in water, stir over high heat until mixture boils and thickens slightly. Stir in sour cream and mint.

Serves 2.

SUMMER VEGETABLE FLAN

Flan can be made up to a day ahead; keep, covered, in refrigerator. Recipe unsuitable to freeze or microwave.

½ cup all-purpose flour
½ cup whole-wheat flour
2 tablespoons vegetable oil
1 egg, lightly beaten
1 tablespoon water, approximately
2 tablespoons (¼ stick) butter
4 green onions, chopped
2 tablespoons chopped fresh basil
2 medium zucchini, sliced
10 lettuce leaves, sliced

FILLING
3 eggs, lightly beaten
8oz container sour cream
½ cup grated cheddar cheese

Sift flours into medium bowl. Add combined oil and egg with enough water to mix to a firm dough. Knead gently on lightly floured surface until smooth, cover; refrigerate 30 minutes. Roll pastry large enough to line 9 inch flan pan, trim edge.

Cover pastry with baking paper, fill with dried beans or rice. Bake in 375°F oven 15 minutes, remove paper and beans, bake further 10 minutes or until golden brown, cool. Melt butter in medium saucepan, add onions and basil, stir over medium heat 1 minute. Add zucchini and lettuce, stir over medium heat about 5 minutes or until vegetables are soft; cool.

Spread lettuce mixture evenly over pastry. Gradually pour filling over lettuce. Bake in 350°F oven about 30 minutes or until set, stand 5 minutes before serving.

Filling: Combine eggs, cream and cheese in medium bowl; mix well.

RIGHT: Summer Vegetable Flan.

Accompaniments

The good, healthy variety here includes mostly salads plus some new and different vegetable dishes. They can be served as appetizers, as accompaniments to a main dish or as main courses, if you like. Many have tasty dressings which add a special zest.

HERBED RICE WITH SPINACH

Recipe is best prepared close to serving time. This recipe is unsuitable to freeze. Suitable to microwave.

1 tablespoon olive oil
1 medium onion, chopped
1 clove garlic, minced
1 cup long-grain rice
1 large vegetable bouillon
    cube, crumbled
2 cups water
½ teaspoon ground turmeric
¼ teaspoon ground nutmeg
½ bunch (10oz) spinach, chopped
3 tablespoons chopped fresh chives
2 tablespoons chopped fresh parsley

Heat oil in medium skillet, add onion and garlic, stir over medium heat about 2 minutes or until onion is soft. Add rice, stir until rice is coated with oil, stir in bouillon cube, water, turmeric and nutmeg. Bring to boil, stir in spinach and herbs.

Transfer mixture to large ovenproof dish (4 cup capacity), cover, bake in 350°F oven about 25 minutes or until liquid is absorbed and rice is tender; stir rice before serving.

Serves 4.

COUSCOUS AND PICKLED GINGERROOT SALAD

Prepare salad close to serving time. This recipe is not suitable to freeze or microwave.

1 cup (6oz) couscous
2oz red pickled gingerroot
1 medium apple
3 green onions, chopped
HERB VINAIGRETTE
¼ cup vegetable oil
¼ cup cider vinegar
¼ teaspoon dried oregano leaves
1 tablespoon chopped fresh chives

Place couscous in large bowl, cover with boiling water, stand 8 minutes. Drain in fine strainer, rinse under cold water. Turn couscous onto tray covered with absorbent paper, dry as much as possible. Rinse gingerroot, drain well. Peel apple and cut into thin strips. Combine couscous, gingerroot, apple and onions in a large bowl, add vinaigrette, toss gently.
Herb Vinaigrette: Combine all ingredients in jar, shake well.

Serves 6.

BELL PEPPER SALAD WITH CRACKED WHEAT

Salad can be prepared several hours ahead; keep, covered, in refrigerator. Add dressing just before serving. Recipe unsuitable to freeze.

3 tablespoons sesame seeds
⅓ cup cracked wheat
2 medium carrots, chopped
2 stalks celery, chopped
1 medium tomato, chopped
1 medium green bell pepper, chopped
1 medium red bell pepper, chopped
1 small cucumber, chopped
DRESSING
2 tablespoons olive oil
2 tablespoons fresh lemon juice
1 clove garlic, minced
1 tablespoon chopped fresh basil

Stir seeds over medium heat in small skillet until lightly browned. Remove seeds from skillet to cool.

Place wheat in small bowl, cover with boiling water, stand 15 minutes. Drain in fine strainer, rinse well under cold water. Turn wheat onto tray covered with absorbent paper. Dry as much as possible. Combine wheat with remaining ingredients in bowl, pour over dressing, toss gently.
Dressing: Combine all ingredients in jar, shake well.

Serves 4.

FENNEL WITH ORANGE SAUCE

Recipe can be made several hours ahead: keep, covered, in refrigerator. Reheat before serving. Recipe not suitable to freeze. Suitable to microwave.

2 medium oranges
¼ cup slivered almonds
1 tablespoon vegetable oil
1 clove garlic, minced
2 medium fennel bulbs, sliced
½ teaspoon cornstarch

Grate enough zest from 1 orange to give 2 teaspoons zest. Cut colored peel from the remaining orange, cut into thin strips. You need about 1 tablespoon strips.

Drop peel strips into saucepan of boiling water, drain immediately. Squeeze enough juice from both oranges to give ½ cup juice.

Toast nuts on baking sheet in 350°F oven about 5 minutes, cool.

Heat oil in medium skillet, add garlic and fennel, stir over medium heat about 5 minutes or until fennel is tender; keep warm. Add grated zest and cornstarch blended with orange juice to pan, stir over high heat until mixture boils and thickens slightly. Pour sauce over fennel, add nuts and orange strips before serving.

Serves 4.

LEFT: Clockwise from left: Herbed Rice with Spinach; Couscous and Pickled Gingerroot Salad; Bell Pepper Salad with Cracked Wheat.

SPINACH AND YOGURT POTATO SKINS

Spinach mixture can be made a day ahead; keep, covered, in refrigerator. Potato skins can be cooked several hours ahead; top with spinach mixture just before baking. We used baking potatoes in this recipe. Recipe unsuitable to freeze or microwave.

4 large potatoes
1 tablespoon vegetable oil
2 teaspoons vegetable oil, extra
1 clove garlic, minced
10oz package frozen spinach, thawed
2 tablespoons plain yogurt
1 cup (2½oz) fresh whole-wheat
   bread crumbs
1 tablespoon butter, melted

Place potatoes on baking sheet, bake in 350°F oven about 1¼ hours or until tender. Cut potatoes into quarters, scoop out the flesh leaving a ¼ inch shell of potato; reserve flesh. Brush potato skins inside out with oil, place onto baking sheet, cut-side-up; bake in 400°F oven about 10 minutes. Chop reserved potato flesh finely.

Heat extra oil in medium skillet, add garlic and drained spinach, stir over heat about 3 minutes or until liquid has evaporated. Remove from heat, stir in potato flesh, yogurt and half the bread

SUMMER SALAD WITH YOGURT CHIVE DRESSING

Salad can be prepared several hours ahead; keep, covered, in refrigerator. Recipe unsuitable to freeze.

⅓ bunch chicory, chopped
1 small cucumber, chopped
1 cup (2oz) watercress sprigs
8 cherry tomatoes, halved
1 medium turnip, chopped
1 medium avocado, sliced

YOGURT CHIVE DRESSING
¾ cup plain yogurt
1 tablespoon fresh lemon juice
¼ cup chopped fresh chives

Combine chicory, cucumber, watercress, tomatoes and turnip in large serving bowl, add avocado and yogurt chive dressing; toss gently to combine.
Yogurt Chive Dressing: Combine all ingredients in small bowl.
Serves 4.

BELOW: Summer Salad with Yogurt Chive Dressing.

crumbs; cool slightly. Combine remaining bread crumbs and butter in small bowl. Spoon spinach mixture onto potato skins, sprinkle with bread crumb mixture, bake in 375˚F oven about 10 minutes or until bread crumbs are lightly browned.
Serves 4 to 6.

ABOVE: From left: Spinach and Yogurt Potato Skins; Fennel with Orange Sauce.

FRUIT AND RICE SALAD

Salad can be made several hours ahead; keep, covered, in refrigerator. Recipe unsuitable to freeze.

¼ cup pine nuts
1 cup (7oz) brown rice
2 tablespoons fresh lemon juice
2 tablespoons vegetable oil
2 tablespoons chutney
2 teaspoons curry powder
1 small carrot, chopped
1 medium apple, chopped
1½ cups chopped pineapple
1 small red bell pepper, chopped
¼ cup chopped dark seedless raisins
¼ cup chopped walnuts

Toast pine nuts on baking sheet in 350°F oven about 5 minutes, cool. Add rice gradually to large saucepan of boiling water, boil, uncovered, 30 minutes or until rice is tender, drain, rinse under cold water; drain. Combine rice, juice, oil, chutney, curry powder, carrot, apple, pineapple, pepper, raisins and nuts in large bowl; mix well.

Serves 6.

BELGIAN ENDIVE AND FRUIT SALAD

Salad can be prepared several hours ahead; keep, covered, in refrigerator. Add dressing just before serving. Recipe unsuitable to freeze.

4 Belgian endive, chopped
3 stalks celery, sliced
1 cup (2oz) watercress sprigs
3 medium oranges, segmented

ORANGE DRESSING
⅓ cup olive oil
¼ cup fresh orange juice
¼ teaspoon prepared mustard
2 tablespoons chopped fresh parsley

Arrange endive on serving plate. Combine celery, watercress and orange segments in medium bowl, serve over endive. Top with dressing.
Orange Dressing: Combine all ingredients in jar, shake well.

Serves 4.

RIGHT: From left: Fruit and Rice Salad; Belgian Endive and Fruit Salad.

BROCCOLI SALAD WITH GARLIC VINAIGRETTE

Salad can be made several hours ahead; keep, covered, in refrigerator. Add dressing just before serving. Recipe unsuitable to freeze.

1lb broccoli, chopped
¼lb cherry tomatoes, halved
2 cups (5oz) bean sprouts
1 cup (5oz) golden raisins

GARLIC VINAIGRETTE
½ cup olive oil
3 tablespoons fresh lemon juice
1 clove garlic, minced

Boil, steam or microwave broccoli until just tender, drain, rinse under cold water, drain. Combine broccoli, tomatoes, sprouts and raisins in large bowl, add dressing; toss gently.
Garlic Vinaigrette: Combine all ingredients in jar; shake well.

Serves 4.

HOT SWISS CHARD AND PEA SALAD

Salad best made just before serving. Recipe unsuitable to freeze. Suitable to microwave.

2 tablespoons sesame seeds
¼ cup vegetable oil
1 clove garlic, minced
½lb small mushrooms, sliced
4 medium Swiss chard
   leaves, shredded
1 cup (¼lb) frozen peas, thawed
2 cups (5oz) bean sprouts
2 teaspoons light soy sauce
2 tablespoons fresh lemon juice
1 teaspoon grated fresh gingerroot

Stir sesame seeds over heat in large skillet until lightly browned, remove seeds from skillet to cool.

Heat a tablespoon of the oil in same skillet, add garlic, mushrooms and Swiss chard, stir over medium heat about 2 minutes or until mushrooms are soft. Add peas and bean sprouts, stir over medium heat 3 minutes. Add combined remaining oil, sauce, juice and gingerroot, stir over medium heat 1 minute.

Sprinkle salad with sesame seeds just before serving.

Serves 4.

ASPARAGUS ZUCCHINI STIR-FRY

Recipe is best cooked close to serving time. Recipe is unsuitable to freeze. Suitable to microwave.

1 bunch (½lb) fresh asparagus
4 medium zucchini
2 tablespoons (¼ stick) butter
3 tablespoons pine nuts
3 tablespoons chopped fresh chives

Cut asparagus into 2 inch lengths. Cut zucchini into thick strips about 2 inches in length. Melt butter in medium skillet, add asparagus, zucchini and pine nuts, stir-fry until asparagus is tender and nuts are browned. Stir in chives.

Serves 4.

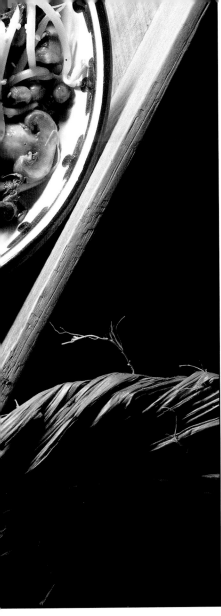

BROAD BEAN AND ZUCCHINI SALAD

Salad can be made a day ahead; keep, covered, in refrigerator. Recipe unsuitable to freeze.

½lb fresh or frozen broad beans
4 medium zucchini, sliced
1 medium red bell pepper, chopped
1 medium onion, sliced
½ cup black olives
7oz feta cheese, chopped

DRESSING
¼ cup olive oil
¼ cup fresh lemon juice
1 clove garlic, minced

Boil, steam or microwave beans until tender, drain; rinse under cold water, drain. Boil, steam or microwave zucchini until just tender, drain; rinse under cold water, drain well.

Combine beans, zucchini, pepper, onion, olives and cheese in large bowl, add dressing, toss gently.
Dressing: Combine all ingredients in jar, shake well.

Serves 4.

CURRIED APPLE AND CELERY SALAD

Prepare salad close to serving time. This recipe is not suitable to freeze or microwave.

¾ cup slivered almonds
4 stalks celery, chopped
2 medium apples, chopped
¾ cup dark seedless raisins
2 tablespoons chopped fresh parsley

CURRY DRESSING
⅓ cup sour cream
3 tablespoons mayonnaise
1 teaspoon curry powder
3 tablespoons fresh orange juice

Toast almonds on baking sheet in 350°F oven about 5 minutes, cool. Combine celery, apples, raisins, almonds and parsley in bowl; add dressing, mix well.
Curry Dressing: Combine all ingredients in small bowl, mix well.

Serves 4.

CRUNCHY RED CABBAGE SALAD

Salad can be made a day ahead; keep, covered, in refrigerator. Recipe unsuitable to freeze.

¾ cup blanched almonds
¼ cup water
1 teaspoon caraway seeds
1 tablespoon tamari shoyu
12 green onions, chopped
1 small red cabbage, shredded
3 stalks celery, chopped
1 red leaf lettuce

Blend or process almonds, water, seeds and tamari shoyu until smooth. Combine with onions, cabbage and celery in large bowl; mix well. Serve over lettuce leaves.

Serves 4.

LEFT: From top: Hot Swiss Chard and Pea Salad; Broccoli Salad with Garlic Vinaigrette. BELOW: Asparagus Zucchini Stir-Fry.

ABOVE: Clockwise from left: Broad Bean and Zucchini Salad; Crunchy Red Cabbage Salad; Curried Apple and Celery Salad.

HERBED MUSHROOM SALAD

Salad can be made a day ahead; keep, covered, in refrigerator. Recipe unsuitable to freeze.

3/4lb button mushrooms, sliced
3 green onions, chopped
1 medium carrot, grated
2 tablespoons chopped fresh parsley
1 tablespoon chopped fresh chives
1 cup (2 1/2oz) bean sprouts

DRESSING
1/3 cup olive oil
1/4 cup fresh lemon juice
2 tablespoons cider vinegar
1/2 teaspoon sugar

Combine mushrooms, onions, carrot, parsley, chives and sprouts in medium bowl, add dressing; stir well.
Dressing: Combine all ingredients in jar, shake well.

Serves 4.

PATTYPAN SQUASH WITH BASIL AND HONEY

Recipe can be prepared a day ahead; keep, covered, in refrigerator. Bake just before serving. Recipe unsuitable to freeze. Suitable to microwave.

1 tablespoon sesame seeds
12 yellow pattypan squash
2 teaspoons olive oil
1 small onion, finely chopped
1 clove garlic, minced
1 tablespoon honey
1 teaspoon light soy sauce
1 tablespoon tahini (sesame paste)
1/3 cup chopped fresh basil

Stir seeds over medium heat in small skillet until lightly browned. Remove seeds from skillet to cool.

Boil, steam or microwave squash until tender; drain, cool. Trim slices from bases so they sit flat; scoop a shallow round from top of each squash. Chop trimmed pieces of squash finely.

Heat oil in small saucepan, add onion and garlic, stir over medium heat about 2 minutes or until onion is soft. Add chopped squash, honey, sauce, tahini and basil, cook over medium heat 1 minute or until heated through.

Serves 4.

CAULIFLOWER IN HERBED TOMATO SAUCE

Recipe can be prepared several hours ahead; keep, covered, in refrigerator. Recipe unsuitable to freeze or microwave.

1 tablespoon olive oil
1 clove garlic, minced
1 medium onion, chopped
2 stalks celery, sliced
1/2 medium cauliflower, chopped
14 1/2oz can tomatoes
15oz can tomato puree
1/2 large vegetable bouillon
**   cube, crumbled**
1/2 cup water
1 tablespoon chopped fresh oregano
1 tablespoon chopped fresh basil
1 teaspoon sugar
1/4 cup grated fresh Parmesan cheese

Heat oil in pan, add garlic, onion and celery, stir over heat until onion is soft. Add cauliflower, undrained crushed tomatoes, puree, bouillon cube, water, oregano, basil and sugar. Bring to boil, reduce heat, simmer, uncovered, about 30 minutes or until mixture is thick and cauliflower is tender. Serve topped with cheese.

Serves 6.

LEFT: Herbed Mushroom Salad.
BELOW: Pattypan Squash with Basil and Honey.

POTATO SALAD WITH CIDER VINEGAR DRESSING

Salad can be made several hours ahead; keep, covered, in refrigerator. Recipe unsuitable to freeze.

¼ cup slivered almonds
5 medium potatoes
3 stalks celery, chopped
4 green onions, chopped
1 medium apple, chopped
1 tablespoon fresh lemon juice

CIDER VINEGAR DRESSING
3 tablespoons cider vinegar
⅓ cup olive oil
2 teaspoons fresh lemon juice
2 teaspoons dark brown sugar
¼ teaspoon dry mustard
1 clove garlic, minced

Toast almonds on baking sheet in 350°F oven 5 minutes until browned; cool.

Boil, steam or microwave potatoes until just tender; cool. Peel potatoes, cut into cubes. Combine potatoes with remaining ingredients in large bowl. Add dressing, toss gently.
Cider Vinegar Dressing: Combine all ingredients in jar, shake well.
Serves 4.

SNOW PEA, APPLE AND NUT SALAD

Prepare salad close to serving time. Recipe unsuitable to freeze.

1lb snow peas
1 medium apple, sliced
1 tablespoon fresh lemon juice
1 cup (3½oz) pecan nuts or walnuts

CHIVE DRESSING
¼ cup mayonnaise
½ cup plain yogurt
3 tablespoons chopped fresh chives

Boil, steam or microwave snow peas until just tender, drain; place in bowl of iced water, drain. Toss apple in juice. Combine all ingredients in a large bowl, add dressing; toss gently.
Chive Dressing: Combine all ingredients in medium bowl; mix well.
Serves 4.

MINTED PARSLEY SALAD

Salad can be prepared a day ahead; keep, covered, in refrigerator. Recipe unsuitable to freeze or microwave.

½ cup cracked wheat
2 cups chopped fresh parsley
4 green onions, chopped
½lb cherry tomatoes, halved
1 small cucumber, chopped
1 stalk celery, chopped
⅓ cup chopped fresh mint
⅓ cup fresh lemon juice
1 tablespoon olive oil

Place wheat in small bowl, cover with boiling water, stand 15 minutes. Drain in fine strainer, rinse well under cold water. Turn wheat onto tray covered with absorbent paper, dry as much as possible. Combine all ingredients in large bowl, mix well.
Serves 4.

BELOW: Cauliflower in Herbed Tomato Sauce. RIGHT: Clockwise from left: Potato Salad with Cider Vinegar Dressing; Minted Parsley Salad; Snow Pea, Apple and Nut Salad.

Desserts

A feature of our desserts is that most are based on fruit with all its luscious flavor and goodness. You have the choice of rich or not-so-rich; hot, cold or frozen (and note the quick-mix pudding to make for Christmas or just a wonderful winter treat). They'd be great as party makers or the perfect finish to a meal.

STRAWBERRY AND LIME SORBET

Sorbet can be made 3 days ahead.

1lb strawberries
1 teaspoon grated lime zest
¼ cup fresh lime juice
⅔ cup sifted confectioners' sugar
2 egg whites

Blend or process strawberries, zest, juice, sugar and egg whites until smooth, creamy and pale in color. Pour mixture into shallow rectangular pan. Cover with foil, freeze overnight.

Serves 6.

BELOW: Strawberry and Lime Sorbet.
RIGHT: Clockwise from left: Chestnut Carob Mousse; Apple Cornmeal Flan; Baked Cheesecake.

CHESTNUT CAROB MOUSSE

Mousse can be made 2 days ahead; keep, covered, in refrigerator. Recipe unsuitable to freeze.

½lb milk carob, melted
1 egg, separated
8oz can chestnut spread
1¼ cups whipping cream

Place carob in medium bowl, cool; do not allow to set. Gradually stir in combined egg yolk and chestnut spread. Beat cream in small bowl until soft peaks form, fold into carob mixture. Pour into 8 serving glasses; refrigerate until set. Serve with extra whipped cream, if desired.
Serves 8.

BAKED PEACH CHEESECAKE

Cheesecake can be made a day ahead; keep, covered, in refrigerator. Recipe unsuitable to freeze or microwave.

¾ cup (1½ sticks) butter, melted
3 cups (¾lb) plain sweet
    biscuit crumbs
3 medium fresh peaches, sliced
¼ teaspoon ground nutmeg

CHEESE FILLING
7oz ricotta cheese
½ cup dark brown sugar
½ cup sour cream
3 eggs, separated
1 tablespoon all-purpose flour
1 tablespoon fresh lemon juice

Combine butter and crumbs in large bowl, mix well. Press evenly over base and side of 8 inch x 3 inch springform pan, refrigerate 30 minutes. Arrange peach slices over base, sprinkle with nutmeg, pour cheese filling over peaches. Bake in 325°F oven about 1 hour or until set. Cool in oven with door ajar; refrigerate several hours before serving.
Cheese Filling: Beat cheese, sugar, cream, egg yolks, flour and juice in a medium bowl with electric mixer until smooth. Beat egg whites in a medium bowl until soft peaks form, fold lightly into cheese mixture.

APPLE CORNMEAL FLAN

Flan can be made a day ahead; keep, covered, in refrigerator. Recipe unsuitable to freeze or microwave.

4 cups milk
¾ cup superfine sugar
3 tablespoons butter
1 tablespoon grated lemon zest
1 cup (7oz) yellow cornmeal
¾ cup golden raisins
⅓ cup chopped walnuts
½ cup heavy cream
1 large apple, thinly sliced
2 tablespoons maple syrup
1 tablespoon superfine sugar, extra
½ teaspoon ground cinnamon

Grease 8 inch x 3 inch springform pan. Heat milk, sugar, butter and zest in medium saucepan, stir over high heat, without boiling, until sugar is dissolved. Bring to boil, reduce heat, stir in cornmeal, cover, cook over low heat 10 minutes, stirring occasionally. Remove from heat, stir in golden raisins, walnuts and cream. Pour into prepared pan, top with apple. Pour syrup over apple. Sprinkle with combined extra sugar and cinnamon. Bake in 350°F oven about 35 minutes or until apple is tender and flan has come slightly away from side of pan; cool to room temperature. Remove from pan, serve with extra maple syrup, if desired.

SUNFLOWER FRUIT SALAD

Fruit salad can be prepared a day ahead; keep, covered, in refrigerator. Add nuts and kernels just before serving. Recipe is unsuitable to freeze.

½lb strawberries, halved
¼lb blueberries
1 medium kiwifruit, sliced
½ medium cantaloupe, chopped
½ cup fresh orange juice
¼ cup slivered almonds
⅓ cup chopped pecan nuts
3 tablespoons sunflower seed kernels

Combine strawberries, blueberries, kiwifruit, cantaloupe, juice, nuts and kernels in large bowl, mix gently.
Serves 4.

BROWN SUGAR MERINGUES WITH CAROB CREAM

Meringues are best filled just before serving. Unfilled meringues can be made up to 3 days ahead; keep in an airtight container. Recipe unsuitable to freeze or microwave.

2 egg whites
½ cup dark brown sugar

CAROB CREAM
¼ cup cottage cheese
1 tablespoon plain yogurt
1½oz milk carob, grated
2 teaspoons honey

Lightly grease 2 baking sheets, cover with baking paper. Beat egg whites in small bowl until soft peaks form. Add sugar gradually; beat until dissolved between each addition. Spoon mixture into large piping bag fitted with ½ inch plain tube. Pipe swirls of mixture, about 2½ inches long, onto prepared baking sheets. Bake in 250°F oven about 2 hours or until firm to touch; cool on baking sheets. Join with carob cream.
Carob Cream: Press cottage cheese through fine sieve into small bowl, stir in yogurt, carob and honey.
Makes about 12

RIGHT: From top: Sunflower Fruit Salad; Brown Sugar Meringues with Carob Cream

QUICK-MIX CHRISTMAS PUDDING

You will need to cook ¾lb pumpkin squash. Pudding can be made a week ahead. Suitable to freeze for up to 2 months. Unsuitable to microwave.

1½ cups whole-wheat self-rising flour
1 teaspoon mixed spice
1 teaspoon ground gingerroot
1 cup (2½oz) fresh whole-wheat
    bread crumbs
1 cup (5oz) chopped dates
½ cup chopped dark seedless raisins
½ cup chopped dried apricots
¼ cup (½ stick) butter
⅓ cup honey
1 cup cold mashed pumpkin squash
2 eggs, lightly beaten

Sift flour, baking powder and spices into large bowl, stir in bread crumbs and fruit. Combine butter and honey in saucepan, stir over low heat until butter is melted; stir into fruit mixture with squash and eggs.

   Spoon mixture into well-greased pudding steamer (7 cup capacity), cover tightly. Place pudding in large boiler with enough boiling water to come halfway up side of steamer. Cover tightly, boil 2 hours, adding more boiling water as it evaporates during cooking time. Serve with yogurt and nutmeg.

Serves 6 to 8.

PEARS WITH APRICOT FRUIT SAUCE

Pears are best cooked just before serving. Sauce can be made several hours ahead; keep, covered, in refrigerator. Recipe unsuitable to freeze or microwave.

6 medium pears
3 cups water
½ cup fresh lemon juice
½ cup sugar
1 cinnamon stick
2 teaspoons grated fresh gingerroot

APRICOT FRUIT SAUCE
1¼ cups apricot nectar
¾ cup water
¼ cup sugar
¾ cup (3½oz) dried apricots
2 teaspoons cornstarch
1 tablespoon water, extra
¼lb strawberries, sliced
¼lb blueberries
1 medium kiwifruit, sliced

Peel pears, leave stems intact. Combine water, juice, sugar, cinnamon stick and gingerroot in large saucepan, stir over high heat, without boiling, until sugar is dissolved. Bring to boil, reduce heat, stand pears in pan, cover, simmer about 20 minutes or until pears are tender. Serve warm with apricot fruit sauce.

Apricot Fruit Sauce: Combine nectar, water and sugar in large saucepan, stir over high heat, without boiling, until sugar is dissolved. Bring to boil, reduce heat, add apricots, simmer 5 minutes. Blend cornstarch with extra water, stir into mixture, stir over high heat until mixture boils and thickens. Add berries and kiwifruit.

Serves 6.

FROZEN COCONUT CREAM AND MANGO CAKE

Cake can be made a week ahead; keep, covered, in freezer.

1⅔ cups canned unsweetened coconut cream
½ cup plain yogurt
3 tablespoons honey

MANGO SORBET
2 medium mangoes
2 teaspoons grated orange zest
½ cup fresh orange juice
3 tablespoons honey
2 egg whites

Line base and side of 8 inch x 3 inch springform pan with plastic wrap.

Combine coconut cream, yogurt and honey in medium bowl. Pour mixture into loaf pan, cover, freeze until partly frozen.

Place mixture into medium bowl, beat with electric mixer until smooth. Spoon evenly into prepared springform pan, cover, freeze 1 hour or until firm. Top with mango sorbet, cover, freeze for several hours or until set. Serve with extra mango, if desired.

Mango Sorbet: Blend or process mangoes until smooth; you need 2 cups puree for this recipe. Combine mango, zest, juice and honey in medium bowl. Pour mixture into loaf pan, cover with foil and freeze until partly frozen.

Place mixture into medium bowl, beat with electric mixer until smooth. Beat egg whites in small bowl until soft peaks form, fold into mango mixture.

LEFT: Quick-Mix Christmas Pudding.
ABOVE: Frozen Coconut Cream and Mango Cake.
ABOVE LEFT: Pears with Apricot Fruit Sauce.

BUCKWHEAT BANANA PANCAKES

Make pancakes close to serving time. Sauce can be made a day ahead; keep, covered, in refrigerator. This recipe is not suitable to freeze or microwave.

PANCAKES
¼ cup buckwheat flour
1 medium banana
2 eggs
¾ cup milk
1 tablespoon fresh lemon juice

ORANGE SAUCE
2 tablespoons (¼ stick) butter
¼ cup sugar
1 cup fresh orange juice
1 tablespoon cornstarch
1 tablespoon water

Pancakes: Blend or process all ingredients until smooth. Transfer batter to medium jug; cover, stand 30 minutes. Pour 3 to 4 tablespoons of batter into heated greased heavy-based small skillet, cook until lightly browned underneath. Turn pancake, brown on other side. Repeat with remaining batter. You will need 8 pancakes for this recipe. Fold pancakes as desired. Serve hot pancakes with orange sauce.

Orange Sauce: Melt butter in a medium saucepan, add sugar, stir over low heat about 3 minutes or until sugar is dissolved and mixture is golden brown. Add juice, stir over heat, without boiling, until mixture is smooth. Blend cornstarch with water, stir into orange mixture. Stir over heat until sauce boils and thickens.

Serves 4.

HONEYED MUESLI AND RICOTTA FLAN

Flan can be made 3 days ahead; keep, covered, in refrigerator. Recipe unsuitable to freeze or microwave.

1 cup (3½oz) untoasted muesli
2 tablespoons (¼ stick) butter, melted
1 tablespoon honey
10oz ricotta cheese
2 tablespoons honey, extra
1 teaspoon grated lemon zest
⅓ cup plain yogurt
1 egg, lightly beaten
¼ cup chopped dried apricots

Lightly grease shallow 8 inch flan pan. Process muesli, butter and honey until muesli is roughly chopped. Press mixture firmly over base of prepared pan, refrigerate until firm.

Combine cheese, extra honey and zest in medium bowl, beat with electric mixer until smooth. Stir in yogurt, egg and apricots. Spread mixture evenly over prepared base. Bake in 325°F oven about 30 minutes or until firm; cool. Refrigerate several hours before serving. Decorate with whipped cream and lemon peel shreds, if desired.

BELOW: Peach and Sour Cream Flans.
LEFT: From top: Honeyed Muesli and Ricotta Flan; Buckwheat Banana Pancakes.

PEACH AND SOUR CREAM FLANS

Flans can be made a day ahead; keep, covered, in refrigerator. Recipe unsuitable to freeze or microwave.

PASTRY
¼ cup self-rising flour
¾ cup all-purpose flour
1 cup whole-wheat flour
5oz (1¼ sticks) butter
2 tablespoons water, approximately
6 medium peaches, sliced

FILLING
8oz container sour cream
1 egg, lightly beaten
⅓ cup sugar
2 tablespoons all-purpose flour
2 teaspoons fresh lemon juice

Pastry: Sift flours into large bowl, rub in butter. Add enough water to mix to a firm dough. Cover with plastic wrap, refrigerate 30 minutes. Divide pastry evenly into 8 portions. Roll out each portion on lightly floured surface until large enough to line 8 x 3½ inch flan pans. Place on baking sheets.

Cover pastry cases with baking paper, fill with dried beans or rice. Bake in 375°F oven 7 minutes. Remove paper and beans, bake further 7 minutes, cool slightly. Place peaches into pastry cases, top with filling. Bake in 350°F oven 35 minutes or until filling is set. Serve flans hot or cold.

Filling: Combine all ingredients in a medium bowl, mix well.

Makes 8.

APRICOT AND PEAR WHIP

Dessert can be made 3 hours ahead; keep, covered, in refrigerator. Recipe unsuitable to freeze or microwave.

3 medium pears, chopped
1 cup (5oz) dried apricots
¾ cup water
1 tablespoon sugar
⅓ cup plain yogurt
2 egg whites

Combine pears, apricots and water in medium saucepan. Bring to boil, then reduce heat, cover, simmer about 15 minutes or until apricots are soft, add sugar; cool to room temperature. Blend or process apricot mixture until it becomes smooth, add yogurt, blend until combined. Transfer mixture to large bowl.

Beat egg whites in small bowl until soft peaks form, fold lightly into apricot mixture in 2 batches. Pour mixture into 6 serving dishes, refrigerate well before serving.
Serves 6.

MAPLE AND BANANA FROZEN YOGURT

Dessert can be made 3 days ahead; remove from freezer 15 minutes before serving. You will need about 3 medium bananas for this recipe.

1 cup mashed banana
¼ cup fresh lemon juice
⅓ cup maple syrup
2 cups plain yogurt
½ teaspoon ground nutmeg
1 egg white

Blend or process banana, juice, syrup, yogurt and nutmeg until smooth. Pour mixture into freezer tray or deep baking pan, cover with foil, freeze until firm. Chop frozen mixture roughly, beat in small bowl with electric mixer until slightly softened. Add egg white, beat until mixture is smooth. Return mixture to freezer tray, cover, freeze until firm.
Serves 6.

FRESH FIGS WITH YOGURT AND COCONUT

Recipe unsuitable to freeze.

1 cup (2oz) flaked coconut
8 fresh figs
1 cup plain yogurt
1 teaspoon grated lemon zest
3 tablespoons honey

Stir coconut over low heat in skillet until lightly browned. Remove coconut from skillet to cool.

Remove stems from figs, cut figs into quarters. Divide figs between 4 dishes. Combine yogurt, zest and honey in small bowl; mix well. Pour yogurt mixture over figs and sprinkle with coconut.
Serves 4.

BELOW: Clockwise from left: Apricot and Pear Whip; Maple and Banana Frozen Yogurt; Fresh Figs with Yogurt and Coconut.

Healthy Drinks

Let's drink to fruit! There's no limit to the fruit you can put together in tangy, tantalizing drinks; just choose lovely glasses to suit the occasion. They're great for children too, as is our luscious sweet shake.

BERRY LIME COCKTAIL

You will need about 12 medium limes for this recipe.

½lb strawberries, chopped
7oz raspberries
1 cup fresh lime juice
1 cup unsweetened pineapple juice
1 tablespoon dark brown sugar
crushed ice

Blend or process all ingredients until smooth; strain before serving.

Makes 4 cups.

CAROB YOGURT SHAKE

⅓ cup plain yogurt
⅔ cup soy milk
1 teaspoon dark brown sugar
2½oz milk carob, melted

Blend all ingredients until they are thick and creamy.

Makes 1½ cups.

Clockwise from left: Carob Yogurt Shake; Berry Lime Cocktail; Apple Blackcurrant Zinger.

APPLE BLACKCURRANT ZINGER

Drink is best made just before serving; mixture will separate on standing.

3½oz fresh or frozen blackcurrants
3 cups apple juice
1 medium banana

Blend all ingredients until smooth.

Makes 4 cups.

ABOVE: From left: Mango Passion Fruit Smoothie; Carrot, Apple and Celery Juice.

CARROT, APPLE AND CELERY JUICE

6 stalks celery
4 medium carrots
5 medium apples
2 teaspoons honey

Have ingredients, except honey, well chilled. Use juice extractor to make juice from celery, carrots and apples, following manufacturer's instructions. Combine juices in large jug, stir in honey.

Makes about 4 cups.

MANGO PASSION FRUIT SMOOTHIE

1 medium ripe mango, peeled, chopped
1 cup soy milk
1 tablespoon honey
1 passion fruit

Blend mango, milk and honey until smooth, stir in passion fruit. Refrigerate before serving.

Makes about 2 cups.

Baking and more

A fabulous feast awaits you in this section. There is a special-occasion torte and rich fruit cake among the cakes, plus scones, muffins, loaves, two particularly good teacakes, cookies and more. Many are packed with fruit; others use vegetables deliciously. Many are simple; some are as rich as you could want.

BELOW: Carob Orange Torte.

CAROB ORANGE TORTE

Torte can be made 2 days ahead; keep, covered, in refrigerator. Recipe unsuitable to freeze or microwave.

½ cup vegetable oil
1 teaspoon grated orange zest
½ cup fresh orange juice
2 eggs, separated
1 tablespoon powdered
   coffee substitute
¼ cup dark brown sugar
¾ cup self-rising flour
¾ cup whole-wheat self-rising flour
1 tablespoon carob powder
1 teaspoon ground cinnamon
⅓ cup coconut

CREAM CHEESE FILLING
8oz package cream cheese
¼ cup sour cream
2½oz milk carob, melted
1 teaspoon dark brown sugar
½ teaspoon grated orange zest

TOPPING
1½oz milk carob, chopped
1 tablespoon butter

Lightly grease deep 9 inch round baking pan, line base with baking paper, grease paper. Combine oil, zest, juice, egg yolks, coffee substitute and sugar in large bowl; mix well. Stir in sifted flours, carob and cinnamon in 2 batches. Beat egg whites in small bowl until soft peaks form, fold into cake mixture in 2 batches. Spread mixture into prepared pan. Bake in 350°F oven about 40 minutes or until firm. Stand 5 minutes before turning onto rack to cool.

Reserve ⅔ cup cream cheese filling. Split cake into 3 layers, sandwich layers with remaining filling. Spread and decorate cake with reserved filling. Press coconut onto side of cake.

Pour topping onto cake, tilt cake until topping covers surface evenly. When topping is starting to set, mark surface into desired number of servings. Refrigerate until topping is firm. Decorate with strawberries, if desired.

Cream Cheese Filling: Beat cream cheese and sour cream in bowl with electric mixer until smooth; beat in carob, sugar and zest.

Topping: Melt carob and butter in bowl.

APRICOT SPIRAL TEACAKE

Teacake is best made on day of serving or can be frozen for 2 months. Recipe unsuitable to microwave.

2 cups all-purpose flour
1½ x ¼oz packages active dry yeast
1 cup warm apple juice
2 cups whole-wheat flour
2 teaspoons grated lemon zest
⅓ cup superfine sugar
¼ cup vegetable oil
¼ cup honey

APRICOT FILLING
1½ cups (7oz) dried apricots
2 teaspoons grated orange zest
½ cup fresh orange juice
½ teaspoon ground cardamom
1 teaspoon vanilla extract
½ cup water
½ cup water, extra

HONEY PECAN TOPPING
1 cup (3oz) old-fashioned oats
1 cup (3½oz) pecan nuts
¼ cup vegetable oil
¼ cup honey
1 teaspoon ground cinnamon

Grease 2 deep 9 inch round baking pans. Sift all-purpose flour into medium bowl, make well in center. Gradually stir in combined yeast and juice; stir until smooth. Cover, stand in warm place about 15 minutes, or until mixture is foamy.

Sift whole-wheat flour into large bowl, stir in zest, sugar and oil. Stir in yeast mixture, mix to a soft dough. Turn dough onto lightly floured surface, knead about 5 minutes or until dough is smooth and elastic. Place dough into lightly oiled bowl, cover, stand in warm place about 1 hour or until dough has doubled in size.

Turn dough onto lightly floured surface, knead until smooth. Divide dough in half, roll 1 half to 10 inch x 14 inch rectangle. Spread half the filling evenly over dough. Sprinkle half the topping over filling.

Starting from long end, roll dough up like a jelly-roll. Pinch dough together at both ends. Place into a prepared pan, joining ends together. Use scissors, snip around top of dough at 1 inch intervals. Cover, stand in warm place about 1 hour or until dough has doubled in size.

Repeat with remaining dough, filling and topping. Bake teacakes in 350°F oven about 40 minutes or until browned. Turn onto wire rack, brush teacake with warmed honey.

Apricot Filling: Combine apricots, zest, juice, cardamom, extract and water in medium saucepan, bring to boil, simmer, uncovered, 15 minutes; cool. Blend or process apricot mixture with extra water until smooth.

Honey Pecan Topping: Blend or process all ingredients until combined.

Makes 2.

CARAMEL TEACAKE ROLL

Teacake can be made a day ahead; keep in airtight container. Teacake can be frozen for 2 months. Recipe unsuitable to microwave.

1 package (¼oz) active dry yeast
1 tablespoon honey
1 cup warm milk
1⅓ cups whole-wheat flour
1½ cups all-purpose flour
¼ cup dried currants
1 egg, lightly beaten
3 tablespoons butter, melted
confectioners' sugar

CARAMEL FILLING
1 cup dark brown sugar
¼ cup water
¼ cup (½ stick) butter
1½ cups (5oz) fresh whole-wheat
   bread crumbs

Combine yeast, honey and milk in medium bowl, mix well. Cover, stand in warm place about 15 minutes, or until foamy. Sift flours into large bowl, stir in currants, make well in center. Stir in combined egg, butter and yeast mixture. Mix to a soft dough.

Turn dough onto lightly floured surface, knead until smooth. Place dough into lightly oiled bowl, cover, stand about 40 minutes or until dough has doubled in size. Turn dough onto lightly floured surface, knead about 5 minutes or until smooth and elastic.

Divide dough in half, roll out each half into rectangle measuring 8 inches x 10 inches. Spread each rectangle evenly with half the caramel filling. Roll up dough from long sides like jelly-rolls, moisten ends of dough with water, pinch ends together. Place on lightly greased baking sheets, allow room for spreading. Cover, stand in warm place about 20 minutes or until increased in size by half. Slash tops of rolls in several places, bake in 400°F oven 10 minutes, reduce heat to 375°F, bake further 15 minutes or until golden brown. Stand on trays 5 minutes before placing onto wire racks to cool. When cold, dust with sifted confectioners' sugar.

Caramel Filling: Combine sugar and water in small saucepan, stir over high heat without boiling until sugar is dissolved. Bring to boil, boil rapidly, without stirring, about 3 minutes or until mixture is slightly thickened. Remove from heat and stir in butter and bread crumbs.

Makes 2.

RIGHT: From top: Apricot Spiral Teacake; Caramel Teacake Roll.

ORANGE PARSNIP CAKE

You will need about 2 medium parsnips for this recipe. Cake can be made a day ahead; keep in airtight container. Cake can be frozen for 2 months. Recipe unsuitable to microwave.

½ cup (1 stick) butter
2 teaspoons grated orange zest
⅓ cup dark brown sugar
2 tablespoons fresh orange juice
3 eggs
½ cup self-rising flour
½ cup whole-wheat self-rising flour
2 cups finely grated parsnip

Grease deep 8 inch round baking pan, cover base with baking paper, grease paper. Cream butter, zest and sugar in small bowl with electric mixer until light and fluffy; add juice, beat until combined. Beat in eggs 1 at a time, beat until combined. Transfer mixture to large bowl, stir in sifted flours and parsnip in 2 batches. Spread mixture into prepared pan. Bake in 350°F oven about 1¼ hours or until firm. Stand 10 minutes before turning onto wire rack to cool.

PEAR AND GINGER LOAF

Loaf will keep for 3 days in airtight container, or loaf can be frozen for 2 months. This recipe is not suitable to microwave.

1¼ cups (7oz) chopped dried pears
¼ cup chopped glace gingerroot
½ cup water
½ cup dark brown sugar
1 tablespoon butter
1¼ cups whole-wheat self-rising flour
1 teaspoon ground gingerroot
½ teaspoon mixed spice
¾ cup slivered almonds

Grease 3½ inch x 10½ inch baking pan, line base with baking paper, grease paper. Combine pears, gingerroot, water, sugar and butter in medium saucepan, stir over low heat until butter is melted. Bring to boil, reduce heat; simmer, uncovered, 2 minutes. Remove mixture from heat, cool to room temperature.

Sift flour and spices into large bowl, stir in pear mixture and ½ cup of the almonds. Spread mixture into prepared pan, sprinkle with remaining almonds. Bake in 350°F oven about 40 minutes or until golden brown. Turn loaf onto wire rack to cool.

RIGHT: From left: Orange Parsnip Cake; Pear and Ginger Loaf; Fig Bars.

FIG BARS

Bars can be made 3 days ahead; keep, covered, in refrigerator. They can be frozen up to 2 months. Recipe unsuitable to microwave.

2 cups (¾lb) chopped dried figs
¾ cup apple juice
5oz (1¼ sticks) butter
¼ cup dark brown sugar
1 cup whole-wheat flour
1 cup (3oz) old-fashioned oats
¼ cup chopped pecan nuts

Grease 7½ inch x 11½ inch baking pan, line with baking paper, grease paper. Combine figs and juice in medium saucepan, bring to boil, reduce heat, cover, simmer about 5 minutes or until figs are tender; cool.

Beat butter and sugar in small bowl with electric mixer until light and fluffy, stir in fig mixture. Add sifted flour, oats and nuts; mix well. Spread mixture into prepared pan. Bake in 350°F oven about 40 minutes or until golden brown, cool in pan.

HONEYED PINEAPPLE FRUIT CAKE

Cake can be made 1 month ahead; keep in airtight container or cake can be frozen for 2 months. Recipe unsuitable to microwave.

2 cups (¾lb) golden raisins
2 cups (10oz) dried currants
2 cups (14oz) glace cherries, halved
1 cup (6oz) chopped dark
**   seedless raisins**
¼ cup chopped glace gingerroot
¼ cup honey
3oz (¾ stick) butter
2 cups unsweetened pineapple juice
1 cup soy milk
2 cups whole-wheat flour
2 cups whole-wheat self-rising flour
2 teaspoons mixed spice

Line deep 9 inch square baking pan with 3 layers of baking paper. Combine fruit, gingerroot, honey, butter and juice in large saucepan, stir over heat until butter is melted. Bring to boil, reduce heat, cover, simmer 5 minutes. Transfer mixture to large bowl, cool to room temperature. Stir in milk, sifted flours and spice in 2 batches. Spread mixture evenly into prepared pan, bake in 300°F oven about 3 hours; cover, cool in pan.

OREGANO CHEESE DAMPER

Damper is best made on day of serving, or damper can be frozen for 2 months. This recipe is not suitable to microwave.

1 cup whole-wheat self-rising flour
1 cup self-rising flour
¼ cup (½ stick) butter
¼ cup chopped fresh oregano
½ cup grated cheddar cheese
¾ cup milk
¼ cup water, approximately
1 tablespoon milk, extra
1 tablespoon grated
**   Parmesan cheese**

Sift flours into large bowl, rub in butter, stir in oregano and cheddar cheese. Make well in center, add milk and enough water to mix to a sticky dough. Turn dough onto lightly floured surface, knead lightly until smooth. Shape into a round, place onto greased baking sheet. Pat dough out to approximately ¾ inch thick and 8 inch diameter. Using a sharp knife, mark into wedges about ½ inch deep. Brush top with extra milk, sprinkle with Parmesan cheese. Bake in 375°F oven about 25 minutes or until lightly browned.

YOGURT AND LEMON CAKE

Cake can be made 4 days ahead; keep in airtight container in refrigerator. This recipe is not suitable to freeze or microwave.

1 cup (2 sticks) butter
2 teaspoons grated lemon zest
1 cup superfine sugar
3 eggs, separated
½ cup coconut
¼ cup packaged ground almonds
3 tablespoons fresh lemon juice
2½ cups self-rising flour
1 cup plain yogurt
HONEY SYRUP
1 medium lemon
1 cup honey

Grease 8 inch fluted tube pan. Cream butter, zest and sugar in small bowl with electric mixer until light and fluffy; beat in egg yolks one at a time. Transfer mixture to large bowl, stir in coconut, ground almonds and juice, then sifted flour and yogurt in 2 batches.

Beat egg whites in small bowl until soft peaks form, fold into cake mixture. Pour into prepared pan, bake in 350°F oven about 1 hour or until firm. Spoon hot syrup mixture over hot cake; cool in pan.

Honey Syrup: Cut peel from lemon, cut peel into small pieces. Squeeze juice from lemon; you will need ¼ cup juice. Combine peel with juice and honey in small saucepan, stir over low heat until honey is melted; do not boil.

SPICY BUTTERMILK CAKE

Cake can be made up to 3 days ahead; keep in airtight container or freeze for 2 months. This recipe is not suitable to microwave.

½ cup (1 stick) butter
¾ cup dark brown sugar
3 eggs
1 cup self-rising flour
1 cup whole-wheat self-rising flour
1 teaspoon ground cinnamon
½ teaspoon ground cloves
½ teaspoon ground nutmeg
1 cup buttermilk
7oz milk carob, melted
1 cup (3½oz) pecan nuts, chopped

Grease 9 inch square baking pan, line with baking paper, grease paper. Cream butter and sugar in small bowl with electric mixer until light and fluffy, beat in eggs 1 at a time, beat until combined between additions. Stir in sifted dry ingredients and buttermilk in 2 batches.

Pour mixture into prepared pan, bake in 350°F oven about 35 minutes or until lightly browned. Stand 5 minutes before turning onto wire rack to cool. Spread cold cake with carob, sprinkle evenly with nuts.

BELOW: Honeyed Pineapple Fruit Cake.
LEFT: From Left: Oregano Cheese Damper; Yogurt and Lemon Cake.

WHOLE-WHEAT RAISIN PIKELETS

Batter can be prepared 2 hours ahead; cook pikelets just before serving. Pikelets can be frozen for 2 months. Recipe unsuitable to microwave.

½ cup whole-wheat self-rising flour
½ cup self-rising flour
¼ cup superfine sugar
½ teaspoon ground cinnamon
1 egg
1 cup milk
1 teaspoon cider vinegar
1 tablespoon butter, melted
½ cup chopped dark seedless raisins

Sift flours, sugar and cinnamon into medium bowl, make well in center. Gradually stir in combined egg, milk and vinegar, stir until smooth. Stir in melted butter and raisins.

Heat large skillet, lightly grease with butter. Drop dessertspoons of batter into skillet from tip of spoon. When bubbles start to appear, turn pikelets and brown on other side.

Makes about 15.

LEFT: Clockwise from left: Whole-Wheat Raisin Pikelets; Pumpkin Squash and Prune Scones; Spicy Buttermilk Cake.
ABOVE: From Left: Tropical Fruit Teacake; Fruity Whole-Wheat Rock Cakes.

PUMPKIN SQUASH AND PRUNE SCONES

You will need to cook about ¾lb pumpkin squash for this recipe. Scones are best made on day of serving. Scones can be frozen for 2 months. Recipe unsuitable to microwave.

¼ cup (½ stick) butter
¼ cup raw sugar
1 egg
1 cup cold mashed pumpkin squash
½ cup chopped pitted prunes
1½ cups self-rising flour
1 cup whole-wheat self-rising flour
½ teaspoon ground cinnamon

Grease shallow 8 inch round baking pan. Beat butter and sugar in small bowl with electric mixer until light and fluffy, add egg, beat until combined. Stir in squash, prunes and sifted flours and cinnamon, mix to a soft dough. Knead gently on floured surface until smooth.

Press dough out evenly until about ¾ inch thick, cut into rounds with 2 inch cutter. Place rounds into prepared pan, brush tops lightly with a little milk. Bake in 375˚F oven about 25 minutes or until scones are browned and sound hollow when tapped.

Makes about 10.

FRUITY WHOLE-WHEAT ROCK CAKES

Rock cakes are best made on day of serving, or can be frozen for 2 months. Cow's milk can be substituted for soy milk, if desired. Recipe unsuitable to microwave.

2 cups whole-wheat self-rising flour
1 teaspoon mixed spice
½ cup (1 stick) butter
½ cup raw sugar
½ cup golden raisins
½ cup chopped pitted dates
3 tablespoons mixed peel
½ cup soy milk
1 egg, lightly beaten
2 tablespoons raw sugar, extra

Combine sifted flour and spice in large bowl, rub in butter, stir in sugar and fruit. Make well in center, stir in combined milk and egg, mix until ingredients are just combined. Drop heaped tablespoons of mixture onto lightly greased baking sheets, sprinkle with extra sugar, bake in 375˚F oven about 15 minutes or until browned. Loosen rock cakes and cool on baking sheets.

Makes about 15.

TROPICAL FRUIT TEACAKE

Cake can be made 2 days ahead.
This recipe is not suitable to freeze
or microwave.

¼ cup (½ stick) butter
½ cup superfine sugar
1 egg
½ cup self-rising flour
½ cup whole-wheat self-rising flour
⅓ cup milk
¾ cup Hawaiian mix
1 tablespoon butter, melted, extra
2 teaspoons superfine sugar, extra
½ teaspoon ground cinnamon

Grease shallow 8 inch round baking pan,
line base with baking paper, grease
paper. Cream butter and sugar in small
bowl with electric mixer until light and fluffy,
beat in egg, beat until combined. Stir in
sifted flours and milk in 2 batches. Stir in
Hawaiian mix. Spread mixture into
prepared pan, bake in 350°F oven about
30 minutes or until browned. Stand 5
minutes before turning onto wire rack.
Brush top with extra butter, sprinkle with
combined extra sugar and cinnamon.

PUMPKIN SQUASH AND HONEY LOAF

You will need to cook 7oz pumpkin
squash for this recipe. Loaf is best made
on same day as serving. It can be
frozen for 2 months. This recipe is not
suitable to microwave.

1 cup self-rising flour
1 cup whole-wheat self-rising flour
½ teaspoon mixed spice
¼ teaspoon ground nutmeg
¼ teaspoon ground cloves
¼ teaspoon ground gingerroot
¼ cup (½ stick) butter
½ cup cold mashed pumpkin squash
½ cup chopped pitted dates
⅓ cup honey
¼ cup milk
1 egg, lightly beaten
2 tablespoons vegetable oil

Grease 5½ inch x 10½ inch loaf pan, line
with baking paper, grease paper. Sift
flours and spices in large bowl, rub in butter. Stir in squash, dates, honey, milk, egg
and oil. Spread mixture into prepared pan.
Bake in 325°F oven about 45 minutes or
until firm. Stand 5 minutes before turning
onto wire rack to cool.

*LEFT: From top: Apple Muffins; Pumpkin
Squash and Honey Loaf.*
*RIGHT: From left: Corn and Peanut Butter
Muffins; Carrot and Walnut Cake.*

94

APPLE MUFFINS

Muffins are best made on day of serving. They can be frozen for 2 months. This recipe is not suitable to microwave.

½ cup whole-wheat self-rising flour
½ cup self-rising flour
¼ teaspoon ground cinnamon
¼ teaspoon ground nutmeg
¼ cup (½ stick) butter
⅓ cup raw sugar
1 cup (3oz) old-fashioned oats
1 medium apple, grated
⅔ cup apple juice
2 eggs, lightly beaten

Grease 12 x ⅓ cup muffin tins. Sift flours and spices into a large bowl, rub in butter. Stir in sugar and oats. Make well in center, stir in apple, juice and eggs with a fork, mix only until combined. Drop heaped tablespoons of mixture into prepared tins. Bake in 375˚F oven about 20 minutes or until golden brown.

Makes 12.

CORN AND PEANUT BUTTER MUFFINS

Muffins are best made on day of serving. Muffins can be frozen for 2 months. This recipe is not suitable to microwave.

1½ cups whole-wheat self-rising flour
1½ cups self-rising flour
¼ cup superfine sugar
¼ cup (½ stick) butter
1 cup milk
10oz can creamed corn
½ cup chunky peanut butter
2 eggs, lightly beaten

Grease 12 x ⅓ cup muffin tins. Sift flours and sugar into large bowl, rub in butter; make well in center. Combine remaining ingredients in medium bowl, add to flour mixture; mix with fork only until combined. Drop heaped tablespoons of mixture into prepared tins. Bake in 375˚F oven about 20 minutes or until browned.

Makes 12.

CARROT AND WALNUT CAKE

You will need 2 medium carrots for this recipe. Cake can be made up to 2 days ahead; keep in airtight container. Recipe unsuitable to freeze or microwave.

1½ cups self-rising flour
1 teaspoon ground cinnamon
¾ cup raw sugar
2 cups grated carrot
½ cup golden raisins
½ cup chopped walnuts
1 cup vegetable oil
4 eggs, lightly beaten

Grease 5½ inch x 8½ inch loaf pan, line base with baking paper, grease paper. Sift flour and cinnamon into large bowl, stir in sugar, carrot, golden raisins and walnuts. Combine oil and eggs, stir into flour mixture. Pour mixture into prepared pan, bake in 350˚F oven about 1 hour or until firm. Stand 5 minutes before turning onto wire rack to cool.

PINEAPPLE DATE BARS

Bars can be made 2 days ahead; keep in airtight container. Bars can be frozen for a month. Recipe unsuitable to microwave.

¾ cup chopped pitted dates
14½oz can unsweetened
    pineapple chunks
1 cup self-rising flour
½ cup whole-wheat flour
1 cup (3oz) old-fashioned oats
¼ cup dark brown sugar
½ cup shredded coconut
¼ cup (½ stick) butter, melted
2 eggs, lightly beaten

Lightly grease 10 inch x 12 inch jelly-roll pan, place strip of baking paper to cover base and extend over 2 opposite sides, grease paper. Combine dates and un-drained pineapple in small saucepan, bring to boil; reduce heat, simmer, un-covered, 5 minutes. Remove from heat, drain, reserving ½ cup juice.

Combine pineapple mixture, sifted flours, oats, sugar and coconut in large bowl. Stir in combined butter, eggs and reserved juice. Spread mixture into prepared pan, bake in 350°F oven about 20 minutes or until golden brown, cool in pan, cut into bars when cold.

BANANA MUESLI MUFFINS

Muffins can be frozen for 2 months. Cow's milk can be substituted for soy milk, if desired. You will need about 2 large bananas for these muffins. Suitable to microwave.

1½ cups whole-wheat self-rising flour
½ teaspoon ground nutmeg
½ cup untoasted muesli
⅓ cup wheatgerm
½ cup raw sugar
¾ cup mashed banana
3oz (¾ stick) butter, melted
2 eggs, lightly beaten
⅔ cup soy milk
2 tablespoons wheatgerm, extra

Grease 12 x ⅓ cup muffin tins. Combine sifted flour and nutmeg, muesli, wheat-germ and sugar in large bowl. Stir in com-bined banana, butter, eggs and milk, mix with fork only until ingredients are just combined. Drop rounded tablespoons of mixture into prepared tins, sprinkle with extra wheatgerm, bake in 375°F oven about 20 minutes or until lightly browned. Makes 12.

RIGHT: Clockwise from top right: Peanut Butter Loaf; Pineapple Date Bars; Date and Citrus Bars; Banana Muesli Muffins.

DATE AND CITRUS BARS

Bars can be made 2 days ahead; keep in airtight container or freeze for 2 months. This recipe is unsuitable to microwave.

½ cup (1 stick) butter
½ cup dark brown sugar
¾ cup water
1 cup (5½oz) chopped pitted dates
½ cup mixed peel
¾ cup whole-wheat flour
¾ cup whole-wheat self-rising flour
½ cup unprocessed bran
½ cup unsalted roasted peanuts
2 eggs, lightly beaten
1 teaspoon vanilla extract

Grease 10 inch x 12 inch jelly-roll pan, line base with baking paper, grease paper. Combine butter, sugar, water, dates and peel in saucepan, stir over heat, without boiling, until sugar is dissolved. Bring to boil, remove from heat; cool in pan.

Sift flours into large bowl, add bran and peanuts; mix well. Stir in combined eggs, extract and date mixture. Spread mixture into prepared pan, bake in 350°F oven about 30 minutes or until golden brown.

PEANUT BUTTER LOAF

Loaf can be made 3 days ahead; keep in airtight container. Recipe unsuitable to freeze or microwave.

½ cup (1 stick) butter
½ cup honey
3 eggs
⅓ cup smooth peanut butter
1 cup self-rising flour
¾ cup whole-wheat flour
½ cup buttermilk

Grease deep 5½ inch x 8½ inch loaf pan, line base with baking paper, grease paper. Cream butter in small bowl with electric mixer until light and fluffy, add honey, beat well. Beat in eggs, 1 at a time, then beat in peanut butter. Transfer to large bowl.

Stir in sifted flours and milk in 2 batches. Pour mixture into prepared pan, bake in 350°F oven about 30 minutes or until firm. Stand 5 minutes before turning onto wire rack to cool.

OATMEAL APPLE PIKELETS

Pikelets are best made on day of serving or can be frozen for 2 months. Recipe unsuitable to microwave.

1 cup self-rising flour
1 teaspoon ground cinnamon
3 tablespoons dark brown sugar
⅔ cup old-fashioned oats
1 egg, lightly beaten
1¼ cups soy milk
1 medium apple, grated
½ cup chopped walnuts

Sift flour and cinnamon into medium bowl, stir in sugar and oats. Make well in center, gradually stir in combined egg and soy milk. Stir in apple and nuts. Cover, stand 10 minutes.

Heat large skillet, lightly grease with butter. Drop tablespoons of mixture into skillet from tip of spoon. When bubbles appear, turn pikelets over, cook until lightly browned underneath.

Makes about 20.

BELOW: From top: Apricot Muesli Cookies, Oatmeal Apple Pikelets.
RIGHT: From left: Caraway Cookies, Apple Apricot Bars, Peanut Coconut Cookies.

APRICOT MUESLI COOKIES

Cookies can be made 3 days ahead; keep in airtight container. They can be frozen for 2 months. Recipe unsuitable to microwave.

1 cup (4½oz) toasted apricot muesli
1 cup (3oz) old-fashioned oats
1 cup (3oz) coconut
½ cup whole-wheat self-rising flour
½ cup raw sugar
¼ cup sesame seeds
1 tablespoon honey
1 egg, lightly beaten
¾ cup (1½ sticks) butter, melted

Combine muesli, oats, coconut, flour, sugar and seeds in large bowl, make well in center. Stir in combined honey, egg and butter. Drop heaped teaspoons of mixture about 1¼ inches apart onto lightly greased baking sheets, press with fork. Bake in 350°F oven about 10 minutes or until golden brown. Cool on baking sheets.

Makes about 45.

APRICOT APPLE BARS

Recipe can be made 2 days ahead; keep, covered, in refrigerator. Bars can be frozen for 2 months. Recipe unsuitable to microwave.

1 medium apple, grated
1½ cups whole-wheat flour
1¼ cups (3½oz) old-fashioned oats
¾ cup chopped dried apricots
½ cup slivered almonds
¼ cup sesame seeds
¼ cup honey
½ cup (1 stick) butter
1 teaspoon grated lemon zest
1 tablespoon fresh lemon juice
1 tablespoon dark brown sugar

Grease 10 inch x 12 inch jelly-roll pan, line base with baking paper, grease paper. Squeeze excess moisture from apple. Sift flour into large bowl, stir in apple, oats, apricots, almonds and seeds; make well in center. Combine honey, butter, zest, juice and sugar in small saucepan, stir over heat, without boiling, until sugar is dissolved, stir into flour mixture. Press mixture evenly into prepared pan. Bake in 350°F oven about 35 minutes or until golden brown. Cool in pan, cut into bars.

CARAWAY COOKIES

Cookies can be kept for 2 weeks in airtight container. Recipe unsuitable to freeze or microwave.

½ cup (1 stick) butter
¼ cup dark brown sugar
3 tablespoons honey
1 egg, lightly beaten
1 tablespoon caraway seeds
1 cup whole-wheat self-rising flour
1 cup all-purpose flour

Cream butter, sugar and honey in small bowl with electric mixer until light and fluffy. Add egg, beat until combined. Add seeds and sifted flours in 2 batches; mix to a firm dough. Turn dough onto lightly floured surface, knead lightly until smooth. Roll out to ⅛ inch thickness, cut into 2½ inch rounds using a fluted cutter, place onto greased baking sheets; prick each round with a fork. Bake in 350°F oven about 12 minutes or until lightly browned. Stand 5 minutes on baking sheets before placing on wire racks to cool.

Makes about 24.

PEANUT COCONUT COOKIES

Cookies will keep for a week in airtight container. Cookies can also be frozen up to 2 months. Recipe unsuitable to microwave.

3oz (¾ stick) butter
¼ cup smooth peanut butter
½ cup raw sugar
1 egg
1 cup whole-wheat self-rising flour
1 cup (3oz) coconut
½ cup unsalted roasted peanuts

Cream butter, peanut butter and sugar in small bowl with electric mixer until light and fluffy. Add egg, beat until just combined. Stir in flour, coconut and peanuts. Roll heaped teaspoons of mixture into balls, place about ¾ inch apart onto lightly greased baking sheets, flatten slightly with fork. Bake in 375°F oven about 12 minutes or until lightly browned; cool on baking sheets.

Makes about 30.

WHOLE-WHEAT BREAD ROLLS

Rolls are best made on day of serving, or can be frozen up to 2 months. Recipe unsuitable to microwave.

2 x ¼oz packages active dry yeast
1 tablespoon sugar
½ cup warm water
3 cups whole-wheat flour
1 cup rye flour
¾ cup unprocessed bran
3 tablespoons wheatgerm
3 tablespoons sunflower seed kernels
3 tablespoons millet seeds
1¼ cups warm milk
1 tablespoon vegetable oil
1 tablespoon milk, extra

Lightly grease 2 x 6 inch x 10 inch loaf pans. Combine yeast, sugar and water in small bowl, cover, stand in warm place until foamy. Sift flours into large bowl, add bran, wheatgerm, kernels and seeds, mix well. Stir in yeast mixture and combined milk and oil, mix to a firm dough.

Turn dough onto floured surface, knead well about 15 minutes or until smooth and elastic. Place dough into lightly oiled bowl, cover, stand in warm place about 40 minutes or until dough is doubled in size.

Turn dough onto lightly floured surface, knead until smooth. Divide dough into 8 portions, shape into long rolls. Place 4 rolls crossways in each pan. Cover, stand in warm place about 40 minutes or until doubled in size. Brush rolls lightly with extra milk, bake in 375°F oven about 30 minutes or until rolls are browned and sound hollow when tapped.

Makes 8.

FRUITY BRAN LOAF

Loaf can be made a day ahead; keep, covered, in airtight container. Loaf can be frozen for 2 months, slice bread before freezing and take out slices as required. This recipe is not suitable to microwave.

2½ cups whole-wheat self-rising flour
2½ cups self-rising flour
1 teaspoon mixed spice
2 teaspoons ground cinnamon
2 cups (10oz) oat bran
1 tablespoon butter
3 tablespoons honey
¾ cup water
½ cup golden raisins
½ cup chopped dark seedless raisins
½ cup chopped dried apricots
1½ cups soy milk

Grease 2 x 5½ inch x 8½ inch loaf pans. Sift flours and spices into large bowl, stir in bran; make well in center. Combine butter, honey, water and fruit in medium saucepan, stir over heat until butter is melted. Remove from heat, stir in soy milk. Stir liquid into dry ingredients in bowl, mix to firm dough (you may need a little extra soy milk).

Turn dough onto lightly floured surface, divide in half. Knead each half until smooth, place both halves into 1 of the prepared pans. Place remaining pan over dough so it is enclosed. Use 2 large metal clips to hold the loaf pans together, or, after placing pans into the oven, weight the top pan with a brick.

Bake in 350°F oven 1¼ hours, remove top pan, return bread to oven about 20 minutes or until it sounds hollow when tapped and is well browned. Turn onto wire rack to cool.

CHIVE AND CORN BREAD

Bread is best when freshly cooked. This recipe is not suitable to freeze or microwave.

½ cup self-rising flour
½ cup whole-wheat self-rising flour
¾ cup yellow cornmeal
1 tablespoon sugar
½ cup chopped fresh chives
½ cup sour cream
½ cup plain yogurt
¼ cup (½ stick) butter, melted
3 tablespoons milk
1 egg, lightly beaten

Lightly grease 3 inch x 10 inch baking pan, line with baking paper, grease paper. Sift flours into large bowl, add cornmeal, sugar and chives, mix well. Make well in center, stir in combined remaining ingredients. Spread mixture evenly into prepared pan. Bake in 375°F oven about 25 minutes or until lightly browned. Turn onto rack to cool slightly before serving.

RYE AND WALNUT ROLLS

Rolls can be made 2 days ahead; keep in airtight container, or freeze for up to 2 months. This recipe is not suitable to microwave.

1 package (¼oz) active dry yeast
½ cup warm soy milk
2 teaspoons treacle
1 cup rye flour
1½ cups all-purpose flour
¾ cup whole-wheat flour
½ cup chopped walnuts
1 cup apple juice
1 egg, lightly beaten
1 tablespoon chopped walnuts, extra

Combine yeast, milk and treacle in small bowl, cover; stand in warm place until foamy. Sift flours into large bowl, add walnuts; make well in center. Stir in yeast mixture and apple juice, mix to a soft dough. Turn dough onto lightly floured surface, knead well about 5 minutes. Place dough in lightly oiled bowl, stand, covered, in warm place about 40 minutes, or until dough has doubled in size.

Turn dough onto lightly floured surface, knead well.

Divide dough into 12 portions, roll each portion into a ball, place close together on lightly greased baking sheet.

Cover, stand in warm place about 30 minutes or until doubled in size. Brush lightly with egg, sprinkle with extra walnuts. Bake in 375°F oven about 20 minutes or until lightly browned.

Makes 12.

ABOVE: Clockwise from left: Whole-Wheat Bread Rolls; Fruity Bran Loaf; Chive and Corn Bread, Rye and Walnut Rolls.

Everyone will enjoy these easy-to-eat morsels, whether you serve them after dinner, between times or in school lunches.

APRICOT AND RICOTTA DATES

Recipe can be made a day ahead; keep, covered, in refrigerator. Recipe unsuitable to freeze.

12 fresh dates, pitted
FILLING
¼lb ricotta cheese
3 tablespoons chopped dried apricots
3 tablespoons packaged ground almonds
1 tablespoon superfine sugar
½ teaspoon vanilla extract
½ teaspoon grated orange zest

Fill dates with ricotta cheese mixture, refrigerate. Slice dates before serving.
Filling: Combine all ingredients in a medium bowl; mix well.
Makes 36.

FRUIT AND NUT CAROB CLUSTERS

Clusters can be made 2 days ahead; keep, covered, in refrigerator. Recipe unsuitable to freeze.

5oz milk carob, melted
1 cup (5oz) chopped dates
½ cup chopped glace apricots
½ cup roasted hazelnuts
2 tablespoons coconut

Combine carob, dates, apricots and hazelnuts in medium bowl; mix well. Drop heaped teaspoons of mixture onto foil-covered tray, sprinkle with coconut; refrigerate until set.
Makes about 24.

CAROB SESAME ROUNDS

Sweets can be made 2 days ahead; keep, covered, in refrigerator. Recipe unsuitable to freeze.

3 tablespoons sesame seeds
1¼ cups (3½oz) coconut
3 tablespoons carob powder
3 tablespoons honey
⅓ cup fresh orange juice
extra coconut

Stir seeds over heat in skillet until lightly browned. Remove from skillet to cool.
   Process seeds, coconut, carob, honey and juice until well combined. Roll mixture into small balls, toss in extra coconut, refrigerate until firm.
Makes about 35.

LEFT: From left: Apricot and Ricotta Dates; Fruit and Nut Carob Clusters; Carob Sesame Rounds.

Dinner Party for 2

Colorful and tasty vegetarian dishes fit perfectly into a smart dinner party, and are simple to prepare. These servings are generous for 2 people, and we give you do-ahead tips to make preparation easy.

MENU

Soup
Pumpkin Squash and Walnut Soup

Appetizer
Nutty Lentil Pastries

Main Course
Baked Eggplant with Cheesy Bell Peppers
Snow Pea Salad with Chili Dressing

Dessert
Rhubarb Souffles with Citrus Strawberries

PUMPKIN SQUASH AND WALNUT SOUP

Soup can be made a day ahead; keep, covered, in refrigerator. Soup can be frozen for 2 months. Suitable to microwave.

1 tablespoon butter
1 medium onion, chopped
1 clove garlic, minced
10oz pumpkin squash, chopped
1½ cups water
1 large vegetable bouillon cube, crumbled
2 teaspoons tomato paste
2 tablespoons chopped walnuts

Melt butter in medium saucepan, add onion and garlic, stir over medium heat about 2 minutes or until onion is soft. Add squash, water, bouillon cube, paste and walnuts, bring to boil, reduce heat, cover, simmer about 30 minutes or until squash is tender. Blend or process mixture until smooth. Reheat before serving. Serve with extra walnuts, if desired.

NUTTY LENTIL PASTRIES

Pastries can be prepared a day ahead; keep, covered, in refrigerator. Recipe unsuitable to freeze. Filling suitable to microwave.

3 sheets phyllo pastry
3 tablespoons butter, melted
2 teaspoons sesame seeds

NUTTY LENTIL FILLING
2 teaspoons butter
3 green onions, chopped
1 clove garlic, minced
1½ teaspoons chopped fresh basil
3 tablespoons red lentils
⅔ cup water
¼ cup Brazil nuts, finely chopped
¼ cup lentil sprouts

Layer the pastry sheets together, brushing each with melted butter. Cut pastry crossways into 6 equal strips.

STEP 1
Divide filling into 6 portions, place 1 portion onto 1 end of each strip.

LEFT: Clockwise from top: Rhubarb Souffles with Citrus Strawberries; Snow Pea Salad with Chili Dressing; Baked Eggplant with Cheesy Bell Peppers; Nutty Lentil Pastries; Pumpkin Squash and Walnut Soup.

STEP 2

Fold corner of pastry over filling to form triangle. Lift first triangle up and over, keeping triangle shape.

Continue folding over to end of pastry strip, trim any excess pastry. Place triangles onto lightly greased baking sheet. Brush lightly with butter, sprinkle with seeds. Bake in 375°F oven about 15 minutes or until lightly browned.

Nutty Lentil Filling: Melt butter in small saucepan, add onions and garlic, stir over medium heat about 1 minute or until onions are soft. Stir in basil, lentils and water, bring to boil, reduce heat, partly cover, simmer about 25 minutes or until lentils are soft and mixture is thick. Remove from heat, stir in nuts, cool, stir in lentil sprouts.

Makes 6.

BAKED EGGPLANT WITH CHEESY BELL PEPPERS

Tomato sauce can be made a day ahead; keep, covered, in refrigerator. Eggplant is best baked just before serving. Recipe unsuitable to freeze. Suitable to microwave.

1 medium eggplant
salt
2 tablespoons olive oil
1 medium red bell pepper, chopped
½ medium green bell pepper, chopped
1 clove garlic, minced
1 sprig rosemary
1 tablespoon chopped fresh basil
2 teaspoons chopped fresh oregano
½lb ricotta cheese
½ cup grated mozzarella cheese
3 tablespoons grated Parmesan cheese

TOMATO SAUCE
1 tablespoon butter
1 small onion, chopped
1 clove garlic, minced
1 tablespoon all-purpose flour
1 cup tomato juice
1 teaspoon chopped fresh basil
½ teaspoon chopped fresh oregano
1 teaspoon dark brown sugar

Halve eggplant lengthways, remove flesh leaving ½ inch shell; chop flesh. Place flesh into colander, sprinkle with salt; sprinkle inside of eggplant shells with salt, stand 20 minutes. Rinse flesh and shells of eggplant under cold water, drain; pat eggplant dry with absorbent paper.

Heat oil in skillet, add peppers, garlic and rosemary, stir over medium heat about 5 minutes or until peppers are soft. Stir in chopped eggplant, basil and oregano, stir over medium heat about 5 minutes or until eggplant is soft, remove from heat; remove rosemary. Stir in ricotta, half the mozzarella and half the Parmesan.

Spoon mixture into eggplant shells, place shells on baking sheet, sprinkle with remaining mozzarella and Parmesan. Bake in 350°F oven about 25 minutes or until shells are tender and filling is heated through. Serve with tomato sauce.

Tomato Sauce: Melt butter in medium saucepan, add onion and garlic, stir over medium heat about 2 minutes or until onion is soft. Stir in flour, stir over medium heat 1 minute. Gradually stir in juice, basil, oregano and sugar, stir over heat until mixture boils and thickens.

ABOVE: Nutty Lentil Pastries.
RIGHT: Rhubarb Souffles with Citrus Strawberries.

SNOW PEA SALAD WITH CHILI DRESSING

Prepare salad just before serving. Dressing can be made a day ahead; keep, covered, in refrigerator. Recipe unsuitable to freeze.

3½oz snow peas
½ Boston lettuce
1 small long thin green cucumber, sliced
½ cup cherry tomatoes
1 small onion, sliced

CHILI DRESSING
¼ cup olive oil
3 tablespoons cider vinegar
1 small fresh red chili pepper, finely chopped
1 tablespoon chopped fresh parsley
1 clove garlic, minced
¼ teaspoon sugar

Steam or microwave snow peas until just tender, drain; rinse under cold water, drain. Combine lettuce, cucumber, tomatoes, onion and snow peas in bowl, add dressing and toss gently.
Chili Dressing: Combine all ingredients in jar, shake well.

RHUBARB SOUFFLES WITH CITRUS STRAWBERRIES

Strawberries can be prepared a day ahead; keep, covered, in refrigerator. Make souffles just before serving. Recipe is unsuitable to freeze or microwave.

¼lb fresh or frozen rhubarb
¼ cup water
1 tablespoon cornstarch
2 tablespoons superfine sugar
1 egg, separated
2 egg whites

CITRUS STRAWBERRIES
2 tablespoons superfine sugar
¼ cup water
½ teaspoon grated orange zest
¼ cup fresh orange juice
¼lb strawberries, halved

Combine rhubarb and water in medium saucepan, bring to boil, reduce heat, cover, simmer about 10 minutes or until rhubarb is soft. Blend or process rhubarb mixture until smooth, push mixture through sieve then return to saucepan.

Combine cornstarch, sugar and egg yolk in small bowl, stir until smooth. Stir cornstarch mixture into rhubarb puree, stir over high heat until mixture boils and thickens, remove from heat, cool 5 minutes. Add 1 egg white to mixture, whisk until combined; transfer mixture to large bowl.

Beat remaining egg whites in small bowl until firm peaks form, gently fold into rhubarb mixture in 2 batches. Pour mixture into 2 greased ovenproof dishes (½ cup capacity). Place dishes in small roasting pan, pour in enough boiling water to come halfway up sides of dishes. Bake in 350°F oven 30 minutes. Serve souffles immediately with strawberries.
Citrus Strawberries: Combine sugar and water in small saucepan, stir over high heat, without boiling, until sugar is dissolved, bring to boil, boil uncovered, without stirring, 4 minutes. Stir in zest and juice, cool mixture to room temperature. Add strawberries, cover and refrigerate until cool.

Here's a terrific variety of tastes and textures, followed by a refreshing bombe and rich truffles.

MENU

Appetizer
Country Mushroom Pate

Main Course
Herbed Nut Loaf with Pimiento Sauce
Sauteed Garlic Potatoes
Cauliflower Fritters with Tahini Sauce
Artichokes with Vegetables Julienne
Whole-Wheat Poppyseed Damper

Dessert
Grapefruit and Apricot Bombe
Peppermint Truffles

COUNTRY MUSHROOM PATE

Pate can be made 2 days ahead; keep, covered, in refrigerator. This recipe is unsuitable to freeze or microwave.

¼ cup (½ stick) butter
1 medium onion, chopped
1 clove garlic, minced
1lb mushrooms, sliced
⅔ cup fresh whole-wheat
 bread crumbs
¼lb cottage cheese
1 tablespoon fresh lemon juice
2 tablespoons chopped fresh parsley

Melt butter in large skillet, add onion and garlic, stir over medium heat about 2 minutes or until onion is soft. Stir in mushrooms, reduce heat, cover, cook gently about 10 minutes. Remove lid, bring to boil, boil until liquid has evaporated; cool.

Blend or process mushroom mixture with remaining ingredients until smooth. Transfer mixture to serving dish. Cover, refrigerate several hours. Serve with whole-wheat melba toast and crunchy fresh vegetables, if desired.

HERBED NUT LOAF WITH PIMIENTO SAUCE

Loaf can be prepared 3 hours before baking. Sauce can be made 2 days ahead; keep, covered, in refrigerator. This recipe is unsuitable to freeze or microwave.

2 tablespoons (¼ stick) butter
1 large onion, finely chopped
2 tablespoons all-purpose flour
1 cup skim milk
2 egg whites
1½ cups (7oz) unsalted cashew nuts,
 finely ground
¾ cup Brazil nuts, finely ground
2 cups (7oz) fresh whole-wheat
 bread crumbs
¼ cup grated cheddar cheese
1 tablespoon chopped fresh parsley
HERB SEASONING
2 cups (7oz) fresh whole-wheat
 bread crumbs
4 green onions, chopped
1 teaspoon chopped fresh thyme
1 teaspoon chopped fresh rosemary
1 teaspoon chopped fresh sage
3 tablespoons chopped fresh parsley
3 tablespoons chopped fresh chives
¼ teaspoon ground nutmeg
2 egg yolks
3oz (¾ stick) butter, melted
PIMIENTO SAUCE
2 tablespoons (¼ stick) butter
1 small onion, chopped
1 clove garlic, minced
14oz can pimientos, drained, chopped
1 tablespoon sugar
¾ cup water
2 teaspoons fresh lemon juice

Lightly grease 6 inch x 10 inch loaf pan, line base with baking paper, grease paper. Melt butter in medium saucepan, add onion, stir over medium heat about 2 minutes or until onion is soft. Stir in flour, stir over medium heat 1 minute.

Remove from heat, gradually stir in milk, stir over high heat until mixture boils and thickens; cool, stir in egg whites, nuts, bread crumbs, cheese and parsley.

Spread half mixture into prepared pan. Top evenly with herb seasoning, then remaining nut mixture, press lightly to level surface. Bake in 350°F oven about 1 hour or until firm. Stand 5 minutes before turning onto plate; sprinkle with extra grated cheese, if desired. Serve sliced with pimiento sauce.

Herb Seasoning: Combine all ingredients in medium bowl, mix well.

Pimiento Sauce: Melt butter in small saucepan, add onion and garlic, stir over medium heat about 2 minutes or until onion is soft. Add pimientos, sugar, water and juice, bring to boil, reduce heat, simmer, uncovered, 1 minute. Blend or process mixture until smooth.

ABOVE: From left: Herbed Nut Loaf with Pimiento Sauce, Artichokes with Vegetables Julienne.

SAUTEED GARLIC POTATOES

Potatoes can be cooked several hours ahead; keep, covered, in refrigerator. This recipe is unsuitable to freeze. Potatoes suitable to microwave.

3lb small new potatoes, halved
3oz (¾ stick) butter
1 tablespoon olive oil
2 cloves garlic, minced
1 tablespoon grated lemon zest
3 tablespoons chopped fresh parsley

Boil, steam or microwave potatoes until just tender; drain well. Heat butter and oil in large skillet, add garlic and potatoes, stir over medium heat about 8 minutes or until potatoes are golden brown. Remove potatoes from pan, combine in large bowl with zest and parsley, toss gently.

CAULIFLOWER FRITTERS WITH TAHINI SAUCE

Fritters are best made just before serving. Sauce can be made a day ahead; keep, covered in refrigerator. This recipe is unsuitable to freeze. Cauliflower suitable to microwave.

½ medium cauliflower, chopped

BATTER
1 cup all-purpose flour
2 tablespoons vegetable oil
½ teaspoon sesame oil
¾ cup water
1 egg white
oil for deep-frying

TAHINI SAUCE
¼ cup tahini (sesame paste)
¼ cup fresh lemon juice
1 tablespoon water
2 tablespoons vegetable oil
1 tablespoon chopped fresh parsley

Boil steam or microwave cauliflower until just tender; drain, cool.
Batter: Sift flour into medium bowl, make well in center. Gradually stir in combined oils and water, mix to a smooth batter. Beat egg white in small bowl until firm peaks form, fold into batter. Dip cauliflower pieces into batter, deep-fry in hot oil until lightly browned; drain on absorbent paper. Serve with sauce.
Tahini Sauce: Combine all ingredients in small bowl, mix well.

ARTICHOKES WITH VEGETABLES JULIENNE

Vegetables and dressing can be prepared a day ahead; keep, covered, in refrigerator. This recipe is unsuitable to freeze.

14oz can artichoke bottoms, drained
1 medium carrot
1 medium red bell pepper
3½oz green beans
CHEESY DRESSING
2 egg yolks
3 tablespoons ricotta cheese
3 tablespoons grated cheddar cheese
1 tablespoon fresh orange juice
1 teaspoon seeded mustard
2 teaspoons chopped fresh thyme
½ cup olive oil

Cut artichokes, carrot and pepper into thin strips about 2 inches long. Cut beans into 2 inch pieces. Boil, steam or microwave beans and carrots until just tender; cool. Combine all vegetables in dish. Serve with dressing.
Cheesy Dressing: Blend or process egg yolks, cheeses, juice, mustard and thyme until smooth. Add oil gradually while motor is operating until mixture is thickened.

WHOLE-WHEAT POPPYSEED DAMPER

Make damper as close to serving time as possible. Damper can be frozen for 2 months. Recipe unsuitable to microwave.

3 cups whole-wheat self-rising flour
1 tablespoon poppy seeds
2 tablespoons vegetable oil
1⅓ cups buttermilk, approximately

Sift flour into large bowl, add poppy seeds, mix well, make well in center. Stir in oil and enough buttermilk to mix to a sticky dough. Turn dough onto lightly floured surface, knead until smooth and round.

Place dough onto lightly greased baking sheet, pat firmly until about 1¾ inches thick. Using a sharp knife, cut a cross in the top about ½ inch deep. Brush top with a little milk, sprinkle with extra poppy seeds, if desired. Bake in 375°F oven about 40 minutes or until browned.

GRAPEFRUIT AND APRICOT BOMBE

Bombe is best made a day ahead; keep, covered, in freezer.

3 large grapefruit
1⅓ cups superfine sugar
1lb fresh apricots, chopped
2 cups milk

Peel and segment grapefruit, discard seeds. Combine grapefruit and 1 cup of the sugar in food processor, process until smooth. Pour mixture into shallow rectangular pan, cover with foil, freeze about 2 hours or until mixture is firm.

Flake mixture with a fork, press evenly over base and side of well-chilled aluminium pudding steamer (6 cup

capacity), cover, freeze until firm.

Process remaining sugar, apricots and milk until smooth. Pour into center of steamer, cover, freeze until firm.

To serve, dip base of steamer into hot water, turn onto dish.

PEPPERMINT TRUFFLES

Truffles can be made 2 days ahead; keep, covered, in refrigerator. Recipe unsuitable to freeze.

7oz milk carob, melted
¼ cup heavy cream
⅓ cup golden raisins
⅓ cup packaged ground hazelnuts
peppermint extract
¾ cup chopped roasted hazelnuts

Combine carob, cream, golden raisins and ground hazelnuts in medium bowl, stir in extract to taste, cover, refrigerate 30 minutes. Roll heaped teaspoons of mixture into balls, toss in chopped hazelnuts, cover, refrigerate until firm. Serve in foil cups, if desired.

Makes about 30.

ABOVE: From top: Peppermint Truffles; Grapefruit and Apricot Bombe.

Buffet Dinner for 20

The food is fabulous in this lavish menu, with dishes reflecting the influence of Indian cuisine; they are all particularly easy for your guests to help themselves

MENU

Appetizer
Spicy Split Pea Bundles

Main Course
Carrot Kofta with Lentil Sauce
Coconut Pilaf
Lentil Dhal
Garbanzo Bean Salad with Chili Lime Dressing
Broccoli and Potato in Spicy Cilantro Sauce
Mushroom and Bean Salad

Accompaniments
Pineapple Sambal
Coconut and Chili Sambal
Tomato Cucumber Relish
Chapatis
Pappadams

Dessert
Fresh Fruit with Gingerroot Yogurt Sauce
Berry Coconut Trifle

SPICY SPLIT PEA BUNDLES

Bundles are best made close to serving time. Filling can be made a day ahead; keep, covered, in refrigerator. This recipe is not suitable to freeze or microwave.

21 sheets phyllo pastry
½ cup (1 stick) butter, melted

SPICY SPLIT PEA FILLING
2 cups (13½oz) yellow split peas
¼ cup (½ stick) butter
1 large onion, chopped
2 cloves garlic, minced
1 tablespoon grated fresh gingerroot
2 small fresh red chili
   peppers, chopped
2 medium tomatoes, peeled, chopped
3 tablespoons tomato paste
1 tablespoon fresh lemon juice
3 tablespoons chopped fresh cilantro

Place 1 sheet pastry on bench, cover remaining pastry with baking paper, then a damp cloth to prevent drying out. Brush pastry lightly with butter, top with another sheet of pastry, brush with butter, top with 1 more sheet of pastry. Cut pastry into 6 equal squares, place a rounded tablespoon of filling into center of each square. Pull up edges of pastry, enclosing filling, carefully twist top into a bundle. Repeat with remaining pastry, butter and split pea filling.

Place bundles onto greased baking sheets, brush all over lightly with butter; bake in 350°F oven about 10 minutes or until golden brown.

Spicy Split Pea Filling: Place peas in large bowl, cover well with cold water, soak overnight.

Next day, add split peas to large saucepan of boiling water, boil, uncovered, about 20 minutes or until tender; drain. Melt butter in large saucepan, add onion, garlic and gingerroot, stir over medium heat about 3 minutes or until onion is soft. Stir in chilies, tomatoes, paste, juice and split peas. Bring to boil, reduce heat, simmer, uncovered, about 5 minutes, stirring occasionally, or until mixture is thick; cool. Stir in cilantro.

Makes 42.

LEFT: Spicy Split Pea Bundles.

BACK RIGHT CORNER: From top: Fresh Fruit with Gingerroot Yogurt Sauce; Berry Coconut Trifle. BACK ROW: From left: Broccoli and Potato in Spicy Cilantro Sauce; Coconut Pilaf; Lentil Dhal; Pineapple Sambal. CENTRE ROW: From left: Mushroom and Bean Salad; Garbanzo Bean Salad

Chili Lime Dressing; Coconut and Chili Sambal; Tomato Cucumber Relish; Chapatis; Pappadams. FRONT ROW: From left: Carrot Kofta with Lentil Sauce; Spicy Split Pea Bundles.

CARROT KOFTA WITH LENTIL SAUCE

Recipe can be prepared several hours ahead; keep, covered, in refrigerator. Recipe unsuitable to freeze. Sauce suitable to microwave.

4lb carrots, finely grated
2 cups all-purpose flour
2 teaspoons ground coriander
½ teaspoon cayenne pepper
2 eggs, lightly beaten

LENTIL SAUCE
½ cup (1 stick) butter
2 medium onions, chopped
2 cloves garlic, minced
⅓ cup chopped fresh cilantro
1 tablespoon garam masala
2 teaspoons ground turmeric
½ teaspoon cayenne pepper
2 cups (14oz) dried red lentils
2 x 15oz cans tomato puree
10 cups water
1 large vegetable bouillon
  cube, crumbled

Combine carrots, flour, spices and eggs in large bowl; mix well. Divide mixture into about 40 equal portions, shape into balls. Place balls on tray, cover, refrigerate 30 minutes. Add 6 balls at a time to large saucepan of simmering water, simmer about 10 minutes or until heated through. Remove with slotted spoon, drain on absorbent paper; keep warm. Repeat with remaining balls. Serve with sauce.
Lentil Sauce: Melt butter in large saucepan, add onions, garlic, cilantro and spices, stir over medium heat about 3 minutes or until onions are soft. Stir in lentils, stir over medium heat 2 minutes, stir in remaining ingredients. Bring to boil, reduce heat, simmer, uncovered, about 30 minutes, or until lentils are soft.

COCONUT PILAF

Prepare pilaf close to serving time. This recipe is not suitable to freeze or microwave.

2 tablespoons flaked coconut
3¾ cups (1½lb) Basmati rice
2¾ cups canned unsweetened
  coconut milk
3½ cups water
pinch saffron powder
½ cup dark seedless raisins
3 tablespoons vegetable oil
2 teaspoons cuminseed
3 tablespoons sesame seeds
½ cup raw unsalted
  cashew nuts

Stir coconut over medium heat in skillet until lightly browned. Remove from skillet to cool.

Wash rice in cold water several times until water is clear; drain. Combine rice, coconut milk, water and saffron in large saucepan, stir over high heat until mixture boils. Add raisins, reduce heat, partly cover, simmer about 10 minutes or until most of the liquid is absorbed. Cover, cook over very low heat further 10 minutes. Remove from heat, leave covered in saucepan.

Heat oil in large skillet, add seeds and nuts, stir over heat until lightly browned. Stir into rice mixture. Spoon hot rice into dish, sprinkle with toasted coconut.

LENTIL DHAL

Dhal can be made a day ahead; keep, covered, in refrigerator. Recipe unsuitable to freeze or microwave.

2½ cups (1lb) brown lentils
2 tablespoons (¼ stick) butter
2 medium onions, finely chopped
2 small fresh red chili peppers,
  finely chcpped
1 teaspoon ground cumin
1 teaspoon ground coriander
½ teaspoon garam masala
½ teaspoon ground cardamom
6 cups water
1 large vegetable bouillon
  cube, crumbled
1 teaspoon ground turmeric

Place lentils in large bowl, cover with water, stand overnight; drain. Melt butter in large saucepan, add onions, chilies, cumin, coriander, garam masala and cardamom, stir over medium heat about 2 minutes or until onions are just soft. Stir in lentils and combined water, bouillon cube and turmeric, bring to boil, reduce heat, simmer, uncovered, about 50 minutes or until mixture is thick.

GARBANZO BEAN SALAD WITH CHILI LIME DRESSING

Salad can be prepared several hours ahead; keep, covered, in refrigerator. Unsuitable to freeze or microwave.

1½ cups (10oz) dried garbanzo beans
1 iceberg lettuce
2 medium green bell
  peppers, chopped
2 medium red bell peppers, chopped
2 medium cucumbers, chopped
5 medium tomatoes, chopped
10 small radishes, chopped
1 medium onion, sliced

CHILI LIME DRESSING
⅔ cup fresh lime juice
1 tablespoon sugar
⅓ cup chopped fresh cilantro
1 small fresh red chili pepper, chopped

Place garbanzo beans in large bowl, cover with water, stand overnight.

Next day, drain garbanzo beans. Add to large saucepan of boiling water, cover, simmer about 1 hour or until tender, drain well; cool.

Combine garbanzo beans in large bowl with remaining ingredients. Line large serving bowl with lettuce leaves, top with garbanzo bean mixture. Pour dressing over salad just before serving.
Chili Lime Dressing: Combine all ingredients in jar; shake well.

BROCCOLI AND POTATO IN SPICY CILANTRO SAUCE

Recipe can be made several hours ahead; keep, covered, in refrigerator. This recipe is not suitable to freeze or microwave.

2 tablespoons vegetable oil
1 tablespoon cuminseed
1 tablespoon ground coriander
½ teaspoon paprika
2lb broccoli, chopped
4 medium potatoes, chopped
4 medium tomatoes, peeled, chopped
¼ cup tomato paste
3 tablespoons chopped fresh cilantro

Heat oil in large saucepan, add seeds, coriander and paprika, stir over medium heat 1 minute. Add broccoli and potatoes, stir over medium heat 1 minute. Blend or process tomatoes and paste until smooth, add to broccoli mixture. Bring to boil, reduce heat, simmer gently, uncovered, about 20 minutes or until potatoes are tender, stirring occasionally. Stir in cilantro just before serving.

MUSHROOM AND BEAN SALAD

Salad can be made several hours ahead; keep, covered in refrigerator. Recipe unsuitable to freeze.

1 cup (5oz) golden raisins
1½lb button mushrooms, sliced
1lb green beans, sliced
1 medium red bell pepper, sliced
½ cup chopped fresh parsley
¾ cup shredded coconut
½ cup vegetable oil
3 tablespoons yellow mustard seeds
¼ cup sesame seeds
⅓ cup fresh lemon juice

Place golden raisins in a small bowl, cover with boiling water.

Combine mushrooms, beans, pepper, parsley and coconut in large bowl. Heat oil in small saucepan, add mustard seeds and stir over medium heat until seeds begin to pop. Stir in sesame seeds, stir over medium heat until lightly browned. Add to mushroom mixture with juice and drained golden raisins, toss gently.

PINEAPPLE SAMBAL

Sambal can be prepared several hours ahead; keep, covered, in refrigerator. Recipe unsuitable to freeze.

1 medium pineapple, chopped
½ cup chopped fresh mint
2 teaspoons grated fresh gingerroot

Combine all ingredients in medium bowl. Refrigerate before serving.

COCONUT AND CHILI SAMBAL

Sambal can be prepared a day ahead; keep, covered, in refrigerator. Recipe unsuitable to freeze.

2 cups (6oz) coconut
2 tablespoons fresh lime juice
6 dried red chili peppers, chopped
4 cloves garlic, minced
1 cup plain yogurt

Blend or process all ingredients until combined. Serve at room temperature.

TOMATO CUCUMBER RELISH

Relish can be made a day ahead; keep, covered, in refrigerator. This recipe is unsuitable to freeze.

1 medium onion, chopped
1 small green cucumber, chopped
2 medium tomatoes, chopped
3 tablespoons chopped fresh cilantro
4 small fresh green chili
　　peppers, chopped
1 tablespoon fresh lime juice
¼ teaspoon ground cumin
¼ teaspoon ground coriander

Combine all ingredients in medium bowl; mix well. Refrigerate relish for 2 hours before serving.

CHAPATIS

Prepare chapatis close to serving time. This recipe is not suitable to freeze or microwave.

3 cups all-purpose flour
1 cup whole-wheat flour
2 teaspoons caraway seeds
½ cup (1 stick) butter
1⅓ cups hot water
ghee

Sift flours into large bowl, stir in seeds, rub in butter; make well in center. Gradually add water, mix to a soft dough. Turn dough onto unfloured surface, knead until dough is smooth and elastic. Cut dough in half, cut each half into 10 even portions. Knead each portion well. Roll each piece of dough into a long thin sausage, roll up into a coil, flatten with hand. Roll coil out to a 6 inch round.

Heat skillet over medium heat, lightly grease with ghee. Cook chapatis 1 at a time. Press edge of chapati lightly with a clean cloth during cooking to encourage it to rise. When golden brown patches ap-pear on bottom, turn and cook other side until golden brown, pressing edge with cloth. Repeat with remaining chapatis.
Makes 20.

PAPPADAMS

Pappadams can be cooked several hours ahead; keep in airtight container. Recipe unsuitable to freeze.

oil for shallow-frying
20 large pappadams

Heat ¾ inch oil in skillet. Add pappadams 1 at a time. Hold under oil with tongs about 3 seconds, turn, cook other side until puffed and lightly browned. Drain pappadams on absorbent paper. Repeat with remaining pappadams.
To microwave: Place 4 pappadams at a time on large plate, slightly overlapping edges, cook on HIGH (100% power) about 1 minute or until puffed on 1 side; turn over and cook further 1 minute or until puffed all over.
Makes 20.

FRESH FRUIT WITH GINGERROOT YOGURT SAUCE

Prepare fruit just before serving. Sauce can be made several hours ahead; keep, covered, in refrigerator. Recipe unsuitable to freeze.

1 medium peach, sliced
2 medium apples, sliced
1 medium pear, sliced
1 medium mango, sliced
3 medium bananas, sliced
½lb strawberries
2 medium oranges, segmented

GINGERROOT YOGURT SAUCE
2 cups plain yogurt
3 tablespoons sugar
1 teaspoon grated orange zest
1 teaspoon grated fresh gingerroot
1 teaspoon chopped glace gingerroot

Arrange fruit on platter. Serve with sauce.
Gingerroot Yogurt Sauce: Combine all ingredients in small bowl, mix well.

BERRY COCONUT TRIFLE

Trifle can be made a day ahead; keep, covered, in refrigerator. Decorate just before serving. This recipe is unsuitable to freeze. Suitable to microwave.

¾lb packaged madeira cake
¼ cup fresh orange juice
½lb strawberries
7oz raspberries
½ cup sugar
3 tablespoons arrowroot
1 cup water
3 cups (9oz) coconut
1 cup confectioners' sugar
5 cups milk
⅓ cup cornstarch
1¼ cups heavy cream
1 tablespoon rosewater

Cut cake into 1¼ inch cubes, arrange over base of serving dish (12 cup capacity). Sprinkle cake with orange juice. Blend or process berries until smooth, strain. Combine berry puree with sugar in medium saucepan, stir over heat, without boiling, until sugar is dissolved.

Blend arrowroot with water, stir into berry mixture, stir over high heat about 2 minutes or until mixture boils and thickens. Remove from heat, cool to room temperature, pour over cake, refrigerate until firm.

Combine coconut, confectioners' sugar and milk in large saucepan, cook over low heat about 15 minutes, stirring occasionally. Strain mixture into large saucepan, discard coconut. Blend cornstarch with cream, stir into milk mixture, stir over high heat until mixture boils and thickens, cool to room temperature.

Stir rosewater into milk mixture, pour over berry layer, refrigerate several hours or until firm. Decorate trifle with extra cream, strawberries and toasted flaked coconut, if desired.

ABOVE: Berry Coconut Trifle served with Fresh Fruit with Gingerroot Yogurt Sauce.

Make Your Own Essentials

Here we show you how to make yogurt, soy milk, cottage cheese, peanut butter and mayonnaise, and grow bean sprouts, letting you have supplies as fresh as you want when you want them. They can all be used in place of commercial varieties suggested in our recipes, if you prefer.

YOGURT

You need to buy fresh yogurt to use as a starter for this recipe. The time it takes to thicken varies depending on the freshness of the starter and the temperature of the mixture and the room. Yogurt makers are available; they take the guess work out of the process. Yogurt can be kept in refrigerator up to 2 weeks. This recipe is unsuitable to freeze or microwave.

2½ cups milk
¼ cup full-cream milk powder
3 tablespoons plain yogurt

STEP 1
Combine milk and powdered milk in medium bowl, whisk well until smooth.

STEP 2
Pour into saucepan, bring just to the boil, stirring. Remove from heat, cool to just above lukewarm (110°F).

STEP 3
Place yogurt in medium bowl, gradually whisk in warm milk. Liquid should be lukewarm (85°F). Strain the liquid.

STEP 4
Pour mixture into 2 clean, warm jars, seal and place in warm position (about 65°F) for 10 hours, without moving; refrigerate mixture several hours before serving.

LEFT: Clockwise from top left: Soy Milk, Yogurt; Cottage Cheese, Peanut Butter, Mayonnaise; Bean Sprouts.

119

SOY MILK

Sweeten milk with sugar or honey, if desired. Recipe can be made 10 days ahead; keep, covered, in refrigerator. Milk can be frozen for 2 months.

⅔ cup (¼lb) dried soy beans
4 cups warm water

STEP 1

Wash beans, place in large bowl, cover with water, cover, stand overnight; drain. Rinse beans under cold water, drain. Rub off skins with fingertips, discard skins.

STEP 2

Blend or process beans until they are finely ground.

STEP 3

Spoon mixture into a fine cloth, tie securely with string. Place cloth into large bowl, cover with the water, squeeze and press for 10 minutes. Remove from bowl, squeeze with hands to remove all liquid. Serve hot or cold.

Makes 4 cups.

COTTAGE CHEESE

Cheese can be made a week ahead; keep, covered, in refrigerator. This recipe makes about 1 cup (½lb) cheese. This recipe is not suitable to freeze or microwave.

8 cups milk
3 tablespoons light sour cream

STEP 1

Heat milk in large saucepan until lukewarm. Place light sour cream in large bowl, gradually stir in milk, cover, stand at room temperature overnight or until mixture is thick. Stand bowl in large bowl in dish containing enough warm water to come up to the level of the milk mixture, stand about 1 hour or until the curd clots, replacing about 2 cupfuls of the water with hot water every 10 to 15 minutes so the that the water remains warm. Occasionally spoon the more solid curd from the outside of the bowl to the center to ensure that the curd clots evenly.

STEP 2

Drop a piece of cheesecloth or muslin into a saucepan of boiling water; boil 2 minutes, wring out, spread cloth over the top of large bowl, spoon curd into center. Gather cloth corners together, secure with string. Suspend the curd above medium bowl, drain 1 hour.

STEP 3

Remove curd from cloth, spoon into small bowl, cover, refrigerate before using.

SPROUTING SEEDS

Many varieties of seeds for sprouting are available from natural food stores, as are sprouter kits for growing them. However, sprouts grow well if you follow the simple method described here. Sprouts keep for about a week in refrigerator after they are removed from their growing area.

STEP 1

Sprinkle 1 to 2 tablespoons of seeds into a glass jar.

STEP 2

Cover seeds with warm water. Cover opening of jar with tulle or fine net, secure with elastic band. Invert jar to drain away water, place jar on side. Rinse and drain twice a day until sprouts have grown to desired size.

STEP 3

Sprouts are usually ready to eat in 3 to 6 days.

PEANUT BUTTER

Peanut butter can be kept in refrigerator for up to 2 months. This recipe is not suitable to freeze.

**½lb shelled, roasted,
  unsalted peanuts
1 tablespoon vegetable oil**

STEP 1

Combine all ingredients in blender or processor, blend or process until as smooth as desired. Refrigerate.

Makes 1 cup.

MAYONNAISE

Mayonnaise is easy to make; the main problem is usually curdling, which occurs when the oil is added too quickly.

If this happens, remove the curdled mixture from the blender or processor to a jug. Place another egg yolk into the blender or processor, add the curdled mixture drop by drop while the motor is operating. Once the mixture is holding together, add the rest of the curdled mixture gradually in a thin stream while the motor is operating.

Mayonnaise will keep for up to a week, covered, in refrigerator. This recipe is not suitable to freeze.

**2 egg yolks
1 teaspoon dry mustard
2 teaspoons fresh lemon juice
1 cup vegetable oil
2 tablespoons hot water,
  approximately**

STEP 1

Blend or process egg yolks, mustard and juice until smooth. Add oil gradually in a thin stream while motor is operating.

STEP 2

Transfer mayonnaise to medium bowl; mayonnaise should be a thick consistency as shown. Stir in a little hot water for a thinner consistency.

Makes about 1½ cups.

Glossary

ARROWROOT: is made from a combination of starchy extracts from the roots of various tropical plants; it is used most commonly for thickening. Cornstarch can be substituted.

BLACK-EYED BEANS: also known as black-eyed peas.

BREAD CRUMBS:

Fresh: use 1 or 2 day old bread made into crumbs by grating, blending or processing.

Packaged: use commercially packaged unseasoned bread crumbs.

BROAD BEANS (fava beans): available fresh, frozen and dried.

BUCKWHEAT FLOUR: flour milled from buckwheat.

BURGHUL: cracked wheat.

BUTTERMILK: the liquid left from cream after separation; slightly sour in taste. Today, it is a cultured product. Substitute skim milk, if preferred.

CAROB: available in blocks and powdered form from natural food stores.

CHEESE:

Cheddar: use a firm, good-tasting cheddar. We used cheese with 33 percent fat content.

Feta: a fresh, soft Greek cheese with a crumbly texture and a sharp, salty flavor. We used cheese with a 15 percent fat content.

Parmesan: sharp-tasting cheese used as a flavor accent. We used cheese with 30 percent fat content.

CHESTNUT SPREAD: puree of sweetened, flavored chestnuts.

CHILI POWDER: the Asian variety of the powder is the hottest and is made from ground chili peppers; it can be used as a substitute for fresh chili peppers in the proportion of ½ teaspoon ground chili powder to 1 medium chopped chili pepper.

CIDER VINEGAR: made from unprocessed apple cider.

CINNAMON: can be bought in dried quills (sticks) or ground form. It is used in sweet and savory recipes.

COCONUT: we used pre-packaged shredded, flaked and desiccated coconut in our recipes.

COCONUT CREAM/MILK: we used both canned coconut cream and milk:

LEFT: From top: Shredded Coconut; Flaked Coconut, Desiccated Coconut.

FLOURS:

We have used several kinds of flour in this book. One cannot be substituted for another and give the same result as the picture. In a lot of recipes we have some white and whole-wheat flour together; this is done to improve the texture of the cake or bread, etc.

Rye flour: is made from ground rye and is low in gluten content.

Self-rising flour: substitute all purpose flour and double-acting baking powder in the proportion of 1 cup all-purpose flour to 2 level teaspoons baking powder, sift together several times before using.

GARAM MASALA: varied
combinations of cardamom, cinnamon, cloves, coriander, cumin and nutmeg make this spice which is often used in Indian cooking. Sometimes pepper is used to make hot variation. Garam masala is available in jars from Asian food stores and specialty stores.

GARBANZO BEANS: cover dried beans well with water, stand overnight. Next day, drain, then boil in plenty of water for around 1 hour until beans are tender.

GHEE: clarified butter.

GINGERROOT:

Fresh: scrape away outside skin and it

one can be substituted for the other. As a rule, the cream is thicker than the milk, but different brands vary. Coconut cream is also available in cartons and blocks of pure creamed coconut.

CRACKED WHEAT: wheat which has been cracked by boiling, then redried; it is most often used in Middle Eastern cooking.

COUSCOUS: a fine cereal made from semolina.

CURRY POWDER: Consists of a mixture of coriander, chili, cumin, fennel, fenugreek and turmeric in varying proportions.

DASHI: is a basic fish and seaweed broth responsible for the distinctive flavor of Japanese food. It is made from dried bonito flakes and konbu. Instant dashi, a good substitute, is readily available. Dashi is used as a broth,

ABOVE. Top Row; From left: Yellow Cornmeal; Cracked Wheat; Rolled Rice.
Bottom Row; From left: Hulled Millet; Couscous; Millet Meal.

BELOW LEFT: Dried Gourd.

BELOW: Clockwise from left: Red Pickled Gingerroot; Fresh Gingerroot; Grated Fresh Gingerroot.

soup or as an ingredient in dipping sauces.

DRIED GOURD: is a white vegetable marrow dried in strips. Available from Japanese specialty stores.

FENNEL: celery-like shoot has delicate, feathery leaves and slight aniseed flavor. Can be used either cooked or raw.

is ready to grate, chop or slice as required.

Glace: crystallized gingerroot can be substituted. Rinse off sugar with warm water; dry gingerroot well with absorbent paper before using.

Red pickled: is dyed and preserved in rice wine and sugar

GREEN ONIONS: also known as scallions.

GROUND ALMONDS: we used packaged, commercially-ground almonds in our recipes unless otherwise specified.

GROUND CORIANDER: seeds of the coriander (or cilantro) plant, which are dried then ground. It is the main ingredient in curry powder.

HAWAIIAN MIX: a combination of finely chopped golden raisins, dark seedless raisins, banana chips, dried papaya, pineapple and coconut. Available from natural food stores.

HERBS: we have specified when to use fresh or dried herbs. We used dried (not ground) herbs in proportion of 1:4 for fresh herbs; for example, 1 teaspoon dried herbs instead of 4 teaspoons chopped fresh herbs.

HOISIN SAUCE: is a thick sweet Chinese barbeque sauce made from salted black beans, onions and garlic.

HULLED MILLET: millet without husks.

KIWIFRUIT: fruit with hairy skin and soft, sweet green-colored flesh. Also known as Chinese gooseberries.

LAVASH: flat unleavened bread of Mediterranean origin.

LENTILS: there are many different types; all require overnight soaking before cooking with the exception of red lentils which are ready for cooking without soaking.

MILLET MEAL: coarsely ground millet.

MUSTARD:

Seeded: French-style mustard with crushed seeds.

Dry: available in powder form.

French: smooth paste with sweet-sour taste.

OIL: we used a light polyunsaturated vegetable oil in our recipes unless otherwise specified. Use the oil of your choice.

OLIVE OIL: virgin oil is obtained only from the pulp of high-grade fruit. Pure olive oil is pressed from the pulp and kernels of second grade olives.

OYSTER MUSHROOMS: also known as abalone mushrooms; are small, fresh cultivated mushrooms.

PASTA SAUCE: commercially bottled Italian-style tomato sauce, usually eaten with pasta.

PEARL BARLEY: barley which has had most of its outer husk removed.

PIMIENTOS: sweet red bell peppers preserved in brine in cans or jars.

PIMENTO (allspice): pimento is the whole fruit; allspice is the ground form, used mostly in savory recipes.

RICE: can be brown or white. Long-grain rice is the most commonly used variety; it is hulled and polished. Brown rice is the natural whole grain before it has been processed; takes longer to cook than white rice.

ROSEWATER: extract of rose petals used to flavor sweet dishes, creams and cakes.

ABOVE: Oyster Mushrooms.

BELOW: From left: Spinach; Swiss Chard.

SNOW PEAS: also known as Chinese pea pods.

SOY SAUCE: made from fermented soy beans; we used the light and dark varieties. The light is generally used with white meat dishes, and the darker variety with red meat dishes. The dark is usually used for color and the light for flavor.

SPAGHETTI SQUASH: type of short vegetable marrow. The flesh resembles spaghetti when cooked.

SPINACH: we used flat-leafed spinach or, if unavailable, use Swiss chard.

SPROUTS: we used mostly mung bean sprouts or alfalfa sprouts. Sprout mixtures or sprout salads are available, if you prefer to substitute them.

ABOVE: Clockwise from left: Alfalfa Sprouts; Mung Bean Sprouts; Lentil Sprouts.

LEFT: Clockwise from top left: Eggplant; Sweet Potato; Zucchini; Green Onions; Snow Peas.

ABOVE: From left: Sesame Seeds; Tahini .

BELOW: From left: Soft Tofu; Firm Tofu; Tempeh.

ABOVE: Clockwise from top left: Confectioners' Sugar; Crystal Sugar; Raw Sugar; Superfine Sugar; Dark Brown Sugar.

SUGAR:
We used coarse granulated white table sugar unless otherwise specified.

Superfine: fine granulated table sugar.

Confectioners': powdered sugar.

Raw Sugar: Natural light brown granulated sugar.

SWEET POTATO: we used an orange-colored sweet potato.

TABASCO SAUCE: made with vinegar, hot red peppers and salt.

TAHINI (sesame paste): a paste made from sesame seeds. Available from natural food stores and specialty stores.

TAMARI SHOYU: a thick, dark soy sauce made mainly from soy beans, without the wheat (used in standard soy sauce). It is used in dishes where the flavor of soy is important, such as dipping sauces and marinades. (Shoyu is Japanese for soy).

TEMPEH: is produced by a natural culture of soy beans; has a chunky chewy texture.

TERIYAKI SAUCE: is based on the lighter Japanese soy sauce; it also contains sugar, spices and vinegar.

TOFU: made from boiled, crushed soy beans to give a type of milk. A coagulant is added, much like the process of cheese making. We used soft tofu and firm tofu. Tofu is easily digested, nutritious and has a slightly nutty flavor. Buy it as fresh as possible; keep any leftover tofu in the refrigerator under water, which must be changed daily.

TOFU SQUARES: available in packets from Japanese specialty stores.

TOMATO PASTE: a concentrated tomato puree used in flavoring soups, stews, sauces etc.

TOMATO PUREE: is canned, pureed tomatoes (not tomato paste). Use fresh, peeled, pureed tomatoes as a substitute, if preferred.

VECON: is a natural vegetable broth paste available in natural food stores. Vegetable bouillon cubes can be substituted; 1 cube to each teaspoon of paste.

VEGETABLE BOUILLON CUBE: contains no animal products but is salty to taste: 1 cube is equivalent to 2 teaspoons powdered bouillon.

VERMICELLI: thin, clear rice noodles.

CUP & SPOON MEASURES

To ensure accuracy in your recipes use standard measuring equipment.

a) 8 fluid oz cup for measuring liquids.
b) a graduated set of four cups – measuring 1 cup, half, third and quarter cup – for items such as flour, sugar, etc.
When measuring in these fractional cups level off at the brim.
c) a graduated set of five spoons: tablespoon (1/2 fluid oz liquid capacity), teaspoon, half, quarter and eighth teaspoons.
All spoon measurements are level.

We have used large eggs with an average weight of 2oz each in all our recipes.

Index

A

Alfalfa Balls with Tahini Sauce 16
Apple and Celery Juice, Carrot, ... 84
Apple and Celery Salad, Curried 67
Apple and Nut Salad, Snow Pea 72
Apple Bars, Apricot 99
Apple Blackcurrant Zinger 83
Apple Cornmeal Flan 76
Apple Muffins 95
Apple Pikelets, Oatmeal 98
Apricot and Pear Whip 82
Apricot and Ricotta Dates 103
Apricot Apple Bars 99
Apricot Bombe, Grapefruit and 112
Apricot Muesli Cookies 99
Apricot Spiral Teacake 86
Artichokes, Cornmeal and
    Herb Seasoned 36
Artichokes with Vegetables Julienne 111
Asparagus Timbales 31
Asparagus Zucchini Stir-Fry 66
Avocado and Garbanzo Bean Salad 47
Avocado and Sprout Salad, Carrot, ... 33
Avocado Spread, Nutty 11

B

Baked Eggplant with Cheesy
    Bell Peppers 106
Baked Peach Cheesecake 76
Banana Frozen Yogurt, Maple and 82
Banana Muesli Muffins 96
Banana Pancakes, Buckwheat 81
Bars, Apricot Apple 99
Bars, Date and Citrus 98
Bars, Fig 90
Bars, Pineapple Date 96
Baskets, Spicy Vegetables in Crispy 32
Bean Casserole, Black-Eyed 50
Beans and Peppers with Polenta
    Triangles 24
Belgian Endive and Fruit Salad 64
Bell Pepper Salad with Cracked
    Wheat 61
Bell Peppers, Fruity Seasoned 46
Berry Coconut Trifle 117
Berry Lime Cocktail 83
Blackcurrant Zinger, Apple 83
Black-Eyed Bean Casserole 50
Bombe, Grapefruit and Apricot 112
Brazil Nut Cutlets with Pimiento
    Sauce 43
Bread, Chive and Corn 100
Bread, Eggplant Spread with
    Lebanese 27
Bread Rolls, Whole-Wheat 100
Broad Bean and Tofu Dip 16
Broad Bean and Zucchini Salad 67

Broccoli and Potato in Spicy
    Cilantro Sauce 116
Broccoli Salad with Garlic Vinaigrette 66
Broccoli Soup, Cream of 4
Brown Sugar Meringues with
    Carob Cream 76
Buckwheat Banana Pancakes 81
Buckwheat Crepes with Spicy Green
    Bean Filling 35
Buttermilk Cake, Spicy 91

C

Cabbage and Pineapple Stir-Fry,
    Honeyed 37
Cabbage Salad, Crunchy Red 67
CAKE
Caramel Teacake Roll 86
Carob Orange Torte 86
Carrot and Walnut 95
Frozen Coconut Cream and Mango 79
Honeyed Pineapple Fruit 90
Orange Parsnip 88
Spicy Buttermilk 91
Yogurt and Lemon 91
Caraway Cookies 99
Carob Clusters, Fruit and Nut 103
Carob Fruit Skewers 11
Carob Mousse, Chestnut 76
Carob Orange Torte 86
Carob Sesame Rounds 103
Carob Yogurt Shake 83
Carrot and Walnut Cake 95
Carrot, Apple and Celery Juice 84
Carrot, Avocado and Sprout Salad 33
Carrot Kofta with Lentil Sauce 116
Carrot Parcels with Basil Sauce 44
Carrot Zucchini Croquettes 20
Cashew Nut Balls, Pasta with
    Tomatoes and 27
Casserole, Black-Eyed Bean 50
Casserole, Eggplant 48
Cauliflower and Celery Pies 41
Cauliflower Fritters with Tahini Sauce 111
Cauliflower in Herbed Tomato Sauce 71
Chapatis 117
Cheese Bites, Olive 14
Cheesecake, Baked Peach 76
Cheese Damper, Oregano 90
Cheese Pasties with Tomato
    Basil Sauce 25
Cheesy Millet Muffins 14
Cheesy Nut Loaf with Tomato Sauce 42
Chestnut Carob Mousse 76
Chicory and Papaya Salad 33
Chili Lentil Loaf 20
Chili Vegetable Hot Pot 44
Chive and Corn Bread 100
Christmas Pudding, Quick-Mix 78
Chunky Vegetable Soup 6
Coconut and Chili Sambal 116

Coconut Pilaf 116
Cookies, Peanut Coconut 100
Cookies, Apricot Muesli 99
Cookies, Caraway 99
Corn and Bean Loaf, Crepe-Wrapped 22
Corn and Peanut Butter Muffins 95
Corn Bread, Chive and 100
Corn Fritters with Minted Sour
    Cream, Curried 17
Cornmeal and Herb Seasoned
    Artichokes 36
Cornmeal Flan, Apple 76
Cottage Cheese 120
Country Mushroom Pate 110
Couscous and Pickled Gingerroot
    Salad 61
Cream of Broccoli Soup 4
Creamed Spinach Pate 12
Crepes, Whole-Wheat Swiss Chard
    and Ricotta 54
Crepes with Creamy Broccoli Filling 57
Crepes with Spicy Green Bean
    Filling, Buckwheat 35
Crepe-Wrapped Corn and Bean Loaf 22
Croquettes with Sweet Dipping
    Sauce, Sweet Potato 30
Crumbed Parsnip Sticks with
    Mustard Yogurt 22
Crumble, Vegetable Nut 30
Crunchy Red Cabbage Salad 67
Curried Apple and Celery Salad 67
Curried Bean and Mushroom Soup 4
Curried Corn Fritters with Minted
    Sour Cream 17
Cutlets with Pimiento Sauce,
    Brazil Nut 43

D

Damper, Oregano Cheese 90
Damper, Whole-Wheat, Poppyseed 111
Date and Citrus Bars 98
Date Bars, Pineapple 96
Dates, Apricot and Ricotta 103
Dhal, Lentil 116
Dip, Broad Bean and Tofu 16
Eggplant Casserole 48

E

Eggplant Chips with Pimiento Sauce 24
Eggplant Spread with Lebanese
    Bread 27
Eggplant with Cheesy Bell
    Peppers, Baked 106
Eggplant with Tomato Sauce,
    Polenta and 51
Eggs, Fresh Herb Seasoned 53

125

F

Fennel with Orange Sauce 61
Feta Cheese Souffles, Zucchini and 33
Fig Bars 90
Figs with Yogurt and Coconut, Fresh 82
Flan, Apple Cornmeal 76
Flan, Honeyed Muesli and Ricotta 81
Flan, Summer Vegetable 58
Flans, Peach and Sour Cream 81
Fresh Figs with Yogurt and Coconut 82
Fresh Fruit with Gingerroot
        Yogurt Sauce 117
Fresh Herb Seasoned Eggs 53
Fritters with Minted Sour Cream,
        Curried Corn 17
Fritters with Tahini Sauce, Cauliflower 111
Frozen Coconut Cream and
        Mango Cake 79
Frozen Fruit Pops 8
Frozen Yogurt, Maple and Banana 82
Fruit and Nut Carob Clusters 103
Fruit and Rice Salad 64
Fruit Cake, Honeyed Pineapple 90
Fruit Pops, Frozen 8
Fruit Salad, Sunflower 76
Fruit Skewers, Carob 11
Fruit with Gingerroot Yogurt
        Sauce, Fresh 117
Fruity Bran Loaf 100
Fruity Seasoned Bell Peppers 46
Fruity Whole-Wheat Rock Cakes 93

G

Garbanzo and Vegetable Hot
        Pot, Spicy 48
Garbanzo Bean and Leek Soup 2
Garbanzo Bean Salad, Avocado and 47
Garbanzo Bean Salad with Chili
        Lime Dressing 116
Gingerroot Loaf, Pear and 88
Grapefruit and Apricot Bombe 112
Green Bean and Coconut
        Cream Soup 2

H

Herbed Mushroom Salad 71
Herbed Nut Loaf with Pimiento Sauce 110
Herbed Rice with Spinach 61
Herbed Seasoned Eggs, Fresh 53
Herbed Tomatoes with
        Cracked Wheat 31
Honeyed Cabbage and Pineapple
        Stir-Fry 37
Honeyed Muesli and Ricotta Flan 81
Honeyed Pineapple Fruit Cake 90
Honey Loaf, Pumpkin Squash and 94
Hot Pot, Chili Vegetable 44
Hot Pot, Potato-Crusted Lentil 46
Hot Pot, Spicy Garbanzo and
        Vegetable 48
Hot Swiss Chard and Pea Salad 66
Hummus Alfalfa Pockets 13

K,L

Kofta with Lentil Sauce, Carrot 116

Lasagne, Vegetable and Tofu 55
Lebanese Bread, Eggplant
        Spread with 27
Leek Roulade with Ricotta Corn Filling 47
Lemon Cake, Yogurt and 91
Lentil Dhal 116
Lentil Hot Pot, Potato-Crusted 46
Lentil Loaf, Chili 20
Lentil Pastries, Nutty 105
Lentil Sauce, Carrot Kofta with 116
Lentil Soup, Sweet Potato and 4
Lettuce Parcels with Carrot Sauce 19
Lettuce Rolls with Beet Salad 41
Lime Cocktail, Berry 83
Lime Sorbet, Strawberry and 74
LOAF
Cheesy Nut, with Tomato Sauce 42
Chili Lentil 20
Crepe-Wrapped Corn and Bean 22
Fruity Bran 100
Herbed Nut, with Pimiento Sauce 110
Peanut Butter 98
Pear and Gingerroot 88
Pumpkin Squash and Honey 94

M

Mango Cake, Frozen Coconut
        Cream and 79
Mango Passion Fruit Smoothie 84
Maple and Banana Frozen Yogurt 82
Marinated Bean Sprout and Sesame
        Salad 32
Mayonnaise, Home-Made 121
Meringues with Carob Cream,
        Brown Sugar 76
Millet and Rice Pilaf, Nutty 29
Millet Muffins, Cheesy 14
Minted Parsley Salad 72
Minted Sprout and Tempeh Salad 53
Mousse, Chestnut Carob 76
Muesli and Ricotta Flan, Honeyed 81
Muesli Cookies, Apricot 99
Muesli Muffins, Banana 96
Muffins, Apple 95
Muffins, Banana Muesli 96
Muffins, Cheesy Millet 14
Muffins, Corn and Peanut Butter 95
Mushroom and Bean Salad 116
Mushroom Filling, Whole-Wheat
        Tartlets with 14
Mushroom Salad, Herbed 71
Mushroom Soup, Curried Bean and 4
Mushroom Spinach Strudel 23
Mushroom Timbales, Spinach and 42

N

Nut Carob Clusters, Fruit and 103
Nut Cutlets with Pimiento
        Sauce, Brazil 43
Nut Loaf with Pimiento Sauce, Herbed 110
Nut Loaf with Tomato Sauce, Cheesy 42
Nutty Avocado Spread 11
Nutty Lentil Pasties 105
Nutty Millet and Rice Pilaf 29

O

Oatmeal Apple Pikelets 98
Olive Cheese Bites 14
Omelets, Pea Souffle 58
Orange Parsnip Cake 88
Orange Torte, Carob 86
Oregano Cheese Damper 90

P

Paella, Vegetarian 27
Pancakes, Buckwheat Banana 81
Papaya Salad, Chicory and 33
Pappadams 117
Parsley Salad, Minted 72
Parsnip Cake, Orange 88
Parsnip Sticks with Mustard
        Yogurt, Crumbed 22
Passion Fruit Smoothie, Mango 84
Pasta Soup, Tomato and 6
Pasta with Fresh Vegetable
        Sauce, Pumpkin 38
Pasta with Tomatoes and Cashew
        Nut Balls 27
Pasties with Tomato Basil
        Sauce, Cheese 25
Pastries, Nutty Lentil 105
Pate, Country Mushroom 110
Pate, Creamed Spinach 12
Patties with Spicy Barbeque
        Sauce, Peanut 50
Pattypan Squash with Basil and Honey 71
Peach and Sour Cream Flans 81
Peach Cheesecake, Baked 76
Peanut Butter, Home-Made 121
Peanut Butter Loaf 98
Peanut Butter Muffins, Corn and 95
Peanut Butter Rolls, Pumpkin
        Squash and 11
Peanut Coconut Cookies 100
Peanut Patties with Spicy Barbeque
        Sauce 50
Pear and Gingerroot Loaf 88
Pear Whip, Apricot and 82
Pears with Apricot Fruit Sauce 79
Pea Salad, Hot Swiss Chard and 66
Pea Souffle Omelets 58
Peppermint Truffles 112
Peppers with Polenta Triangles,
        Beans and 24
Pies, Cauliflower and Celery 41
Pikelets, Oatmeal Apple 98
Pikelets, Rye Savory 13
Pikelets, Whole-Wheat Raisin 93
Pilaf, Coconut 116
Pineapple Date Bars 96
Pineapple Fruit Cake, Honeyed 90
Pineapple Sambal 116
Pita Pizzas, Tomato and Onion 13
Pockets, Hummus Alfalfa 13
Pockets, Vegetable Tofu 19
Polenta and Eggplant with
        Tomato Sauce 51
Polenta Triangles, Beans and
        Peppers with 24
Potato-Crusted Lentil Hot Pot 46
Potatoes, Sauteed Garlic 111
Potato in Spicy Cilantro Sauce,
        Broccoli and 116
Potato Salad with Cider
        Vinegar Dressing 72
Potato Skins, Spinach and Yogurt 62

Prune Scones, Pumpkin Squash and 93
Pudding, Quick-Mix Christmas 78
Pumpkin Pasta with Fresh
    Vegetable Sauce 38
Pumpkin Squash and Honey Loaf 94
Pumpkin Squash and Peanut
    Butter Rolls 11
Pumpkin Squash and Prune Scones 93
Pumpkin Squash and Walnut Soup 105

Q, R

Quick-Mix Christmas Pudding 78

Raisin Pikelets, Whole-Wheat 93
Ravioli with Eggplant Filling,
    Whole-Wheat 39
Red Cabbage Salad, Crunchy 67
Relish, Tomato Cucumber 117
Rhubarb Souffles with Citrus
    Strawberries...................................... 107
Rice Pilaf, Nutty Millet and 29
Rice Salad, Fruit and 64
Rice with Spinach, Herbed 61
Ricotta Crepes, Whole-Wheat Swiss
    Chard and 54
Ricotta Dates, Apricot and 103
Ricotta Flan, Honeyed Muesli and 81
Rissoles with Plum Sauce, Vegetable 52
Rock Cakes, Fruity Whole-Wheat 93
Rolls, Pumpkin Squash and
    Peanut Butter 11
Roulade with Ricotta Corn
    Filling, Leek 47
Rye and Walnut Rolls 100
Rye Savory Pikelets 13

S

SALAD
Avocado and Garbanzo Bean 47
Belgian Endive and Fruit 64
Bell Pepper and Cracked Wheat 61
Broad Bean and Zucchini 67
Broccoli with Garlic Vinaigrette 66
Carrot, Avocado and Sprout 33
Chicory and Papaya 33
Crunchy Red Cabbage 67
Curried Apple and Celery 67
Fruit and Rice 64
Garbanzo Bean, with Chili
    Lime Dressing 116
Herbed Mushroom 71
Hot Swiss Chard and Pea 66
Lettuce Rolls with Beet 41
Marinated Bean Sprout and Sesame 32
Minted Parsley 72
Minted Sprout and Tempeh 53
Mushroom and Bean 116
Potato, with Cider Vinegar Dressing 72
Snow Pea, Apple and Nut 72
Snow Pea, with Chili Dressing 107
Sunflower Fruit 76
Summer, with Yogurt and
    Chive Dressing 63
Sauteed Garlic Potatoes 111
Scones, Pumpkin Squash and Prune 93
Sesame Rounds, Carob 103
Sesame Tartlets, Tofu and 30
Snow Pea, Apple and Nut Salad 72
Snow Pea Salad with Chili Dressing 107
Sorbet, Strawberry and Lime 74

Souffle Omelets, Pea 58
Souffles with Citrus Strawberries,
    Rhubarb 107
Souffles, Zucchini and Feta Cheese 33
SOUP
Chunky Vegetable 6
Cream of Broccoli 4
Curried Bean and Mushroom 4
Garbanzo Bean and Leek 2
Green Bean and Coconut Cream 2
Pumpkin Squash and Walnut 105
Sweet Potato and Lentil 4
Tomato and Pasta.................................... 6
Vegetable and Barley 2
Soy Milk 120
Spaghetti Squash with Broccoli Sauce 29
Spicy Buttermilk Cake 91
Spicy Garbanzo and Vegetable
    Hot Pot 48
Spicy Split Pea Bundles 113
Spicy Vegetables in Crispy Baskets 32
Spinach and Mushroom Timbales 42
Spinach and Yogurt Potato Skins 62
Spinach Pate, Creamed 12
Spinach Strudel, Mushroom 23
Split Pea Bundles, Spicy 113
Spread, Nutty Avocado 11
Spread with Lebanese Bread,
    Eggplant 27
Sprout and Tempeh Salad, Minted 53
Sprouting Seeds 120
Sprout Salad, Carrot, Avocado and 33
Squash with Broccoli Sauce,
    Spaghetti 29
Stir-Fry, Asparagus Zucchini 66
Stir-Fry, Honeyed Cabbage and
    Pineapple 37
Strawberry and Lime Sorbet 74
Strudel, Mushroom Spinach 23
Summer Salad with Yogurt
    Chive Dressing 63
Summer Vegetable Flan 58
Sunflower Fruit Salad 76
Sweet Corn Waffles with Chutney
    and Salad 13
Sweet Potato and Lentil Soup 4
Sweet Potato Croquettes with Sweet
    Dipping Sauce 30
Swiss Chard and Pea Salad, Hot 66
Swiss Chard and Ricotta Crepes,
    Whole-Wheat 54

T

Tahini Sauce, Alfalfa Balls with 16
Tartlets with Mushroom Filling,
    Whole-Wheat 14
Tartlets, Tofu and Sesame 30
Teacake, Apricot Spiral............................ 86
Teacake Roll, Caramel 86
Teacake, Tropical Fruit 94
Tempeh Salad, Minted Sprout and 53
Timbales, Asparagus 31
Timbales, Spinach and Mushroom 42
Tofu and Sesame Tartlets 30
Tofu Dip, Broad Bean and 16
Tofu Lasagne, Vegetable and 55
Tofu Pockets, Vegetable 19
Tomato and Onion Pita Pizzas 13
Tomato and Pasta Soup 6
Tomato Cucumber Relish 117
Tomatoes and Cashew Nut Balls,
    Pasta with 27
Tomatoes with Cracked Wheat,
    Herbed 31

Torte, Carob Orange 86
Trifle, Berry Coconut 117
Tropical Fruit Teacake 94
Tropical Mix 8
Truffles, Peppermint 112

V

Vegetable and Barley Soup 2
Vegetable and Tofu Lasagne 55
Vegetable Flan, Summer 58
Vegetable Hot Pot, Chili 44
Vegetable Hot Pot, Spicy
    Garbanzo and 48
Vegetable Nut Crumble 30
Vegetable Parcels with Yogurt Sauce 53
Vegetable Rissoles with Plum Sauce 52
Vegetable Soup, Chunky 6
Vegetables in Crispy Baskets, Spicy 32
Vegetables Julienne, Artichokes with 111
Vegetables with Lemon
    Gingerroot Sauce 27
Vegetable Tofu Pockets 19
Vegetarian Paella 27
Vinaigrette, Broccoli Salad with Garlic 66

W

Waffles with Chutney and Salad,
    Sweet Corn 13
Walnut Rolls, Rye and 100
Walnut Soup, Pumpkin Squash and 105
Whole-Wheat Bread Rolls 100
Whole-Wheat Poppyseed Damper 111
Whole-Wheat Raisin Pikelets 93
Whole-Wheat Ravioli with
    Eggplant Filling 39
Whole-Wheat Swiss Chard and
    Ricotta Crepes 54
Whole-Wheat Tartlets with
    Mushroom Filling 14

Y, Z

Yogurt and Lemon Cake........................... 91
Yogurt, Home-Made 119
Yogurt, Maple and Banana Frozen 82

Zucchini and Feta Cheese Souffles 33
Zucchini Croquettes, Carrot 20
Zucchini Salad, Broad Bean and 67
Zucchini Stir-Fry, Asparagus 66

Salads

Sensational recipes for all occasions

COUNTRY COOKING

Healthy Heart Cookbook

VEGETARIAN COOKING

THE BEST SEAFOOD RECIPES

Italian COOKING CLASS COOKBOOK

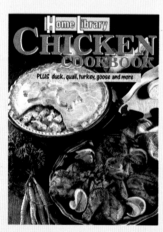

CHICKEN COOKBOOK

PLUS duck, quail, turkey, goose and more

PASTA COOKBOOK

More than 170 recipes

CHINESE COOKING CLASS COOKBOOK

STARTERS AND SOUPS

BEGINNERS' COOKBOOK

FINGER FOOD

Best ever party food
Tempting hot and cold savouries
Do ahead and freezing tips